Texas High School Hotshots

The Stars Before They Were Stars

Alan Burton

Republic of Texas Press
Plano, Texas

Library of Congress Cataloging-in-Publication Data

Burton, Alan, 1956-.
  Texas high school hotshots : the stars before they were stars
  / Alan Burton.
      p.   cm.
  Includes indexes.
  ISBN 1-55622-898-8 (alk. paper)
  1. High school students—Texas—Biography.   2. High
  schools—Texas—History.   I. Title.

  LA2315.T4 B87 2002
  373.118'092'2764—dc21   2002005914

Republic of Texas Press is an imprint of Wordware Publishing, Inc.
No part of this book may be reproduced in any form or by
any means without permission in writing from
Wordware Publishing, Inc.

Printed in the United States of America

ISBN 1-55622-898-8
10 9 8 7 6 5 4 3 2 1
0210

All inquiries for volume purchases of this book should be addressed to Wordware
Publishing, Inc., at 2320 Los Rios Boulevard, Plano, Texas 75074. Telephone inquiries
may be made by calling:

                              (972) 423-0090

To my daughter, Katie

Other books by Alan Burton:

'til the fat lady sings: Classic Texas Sports Quotes
Texas Tech University Press

rave on: Classic Texas Music Quotes
Texas Tech University Press

Contents

                                              Page

Acknowledgments vii

Orientation 1

Freshman
   West Texas (Friday Night Lights) 7

Sophomore
   North Texas (Heroes and Villains) 45

Junior
   East Texas (Reform School) 85

Senior
   Central Texas (All the Way with LBJ) 109

Graduate
   South Texas (Beatniks, Jocks, and 127
      That's the Way It Is)

Continuing Education 169

Sources 187

Index by Person 197

Index by High School 201

Acknowledgments

Texas High School Hotshots was made possible through the cooperation and assistance of many people to whom I am extremely grateful.

First of all, I would like to thank my wife, Michelle, and my daughter, Katie, for their patience and understanding. Michelle did a tremendous amount of typing on the manuscript. As always, Katie provided much needed support and inspiration.

Next, I would like to thank all of those great Texas high school librarians who took the time out of their busy schedules to track down yearbooks and pictures for me — you are the greatest! Also, a big thanks to the celebrities who took the time to send me recent photos.

I know I'm going to miss someone, but here goes my individual list of thank-yous for *Texas High School Hotshots*:

Red Adair, Donny Anderson, Jane Arnett, Karen Barber, Raymond Berry, Mike Biggs, Edie Brickell, Willie Brown, Brian Buntz, Tracy Byrd, Eric Capper, Liz Carpenter, Kathy Carrington, Ernest Cerda Jr., Katherine Cernosek, Mark Chesnutt, Janet Ciaccio, Lori Clark, Mary Clayton, Van Cliburn, Rita Cockerell, Moisann Calderon-Lee, Charles and Lynette Coody, Dr. Denton Cooley, Barry Corbin, Ponce Cruse, Joy Earhart, Morgan Fairchild, Betty Fischer, Paggy Gaines, Larry Gatlin, Larry Hagman, Maria Hinojosa, Dan Hoke, Ray Wylie Hubbard, Karen Hughes, Sen. Kay Bailey Hutchison, Don January, Glen D. Johnson, Susan Keeling, Larry Koeninger, Julie Kretschmer, Jim Lehrer, Justin Leonard, Guy V. Lewis, Trini Lopez, Sandra Lusk, Donna Lyday, J. D. Mayo, N. McClung, Martha McConaughey, Larry McMurtry, Jack Mildren, G. A. Moore, Jr., Michael Martin Murphey, Willie Nelson, Tommy Nobis, Theresa Ochoa, Carrie Jo Parmley, Bill Paxton, Jewell Perry, Gov. Rick Perry, Ronnie Perry, Karen Pevehouse, Teresa Price, Phylicia Rashad, Aban Rustomji, Susan Rhoads, Anne

Rice, Jeannie C. Riley, Kim Rogers, Johnny Rutherford, Mike Sandberg, Ann Sciba, Mike Singletary, Jaclyn Smith, Liz Smith, Aaron Spelling, Joyce Springer, Rep. Charles Stenholm, Betty Sterrett, Glenda Stevens, Julia Stewart, Susan Swain, Y. A. Tittle, Judy Todd, Tommy Tune, Jack Valenti, Vona Van Cleef, Betty Vest, Randy Vonderheid, Kent Waldrep, Larry Watkins, Skip Watson, G. Wells, Dr. Billy Wilbanks, Jack Windlow, David Woo, Gordon Wood, and Sue Worthy.

Also a special thanks to Jostens (Mark Cassutt) and Taylor Publishing Company (Pam Shoemake) for their assistance. Last, but certainly not least, I would like to thank Ginnie Bivona, Martha McCuller, and Paula Price at Republic of Texas Press for their support and encouragement on this project.

Sulphur Springs 1952
Yearbook

"All the world's a stage"-----Sulphur Springs High School has been our stage. Our life at S.S.H.S. is but one act of the great drama in which we will play a part after our school years are over. Here we have experienced all emotions--happiness, romance, and adventure; tears, defeat, and sadness. But here we have gained some of our most precious memories.

The theme of your '52 Cat's Paw is that of a drama. In presenting this drama of 1951-1952, we have striven to portray realistically the scenes of our school year and to help you preserve those wonderful memories of your days at S.S.H.S.

Orientation

"I came back revved up to do well in my senior year, but I couldn't sustain the summer's high. Circumstances never really allowed the inner me to come through with any sense of strength or character. The most devastating example was when the yearbook came out, always a big deal. I wanted to have a yearbook-signing party at home: I had never given a party, other than having the fellowship over a couple of times. Mom helped me organize it, but when the day came, nobody showed up. It was pretty sad. Mom just ached for me; we never talked about it, but I could see how badly she felt. While I was still sitting there in the mounting gloom, a call came from one of my friends. All the kids were over at Stormy Taylor's house and why didn't I come over. Believe it or not, that kind of eased the pain some, but I wouldn't go; I couldn't."

— John Denver (Fort Worth Arlington Heights, '61) in his autobiography, *Take Me Home*

There is no more enduring high school tradition than the annual or yearbook. The first high school yearbook was published in Waterville, N.Y., in 1845. The "modern" yearbook began to take shape in 1880. Yearbooks during this era typically featured posed photographs and illustrations.

From the simple early day annuals to today's sophisticated, computerized, and colorful yearbooks, these documents serve to chronicle the history of "the good old days."

Traditionally, yearbooks, in most cases, have served four functions:

1. History book. Yearbooks give a complete history of one school year. The activities and issues of the year are related through the stories. The photos capture the appearance of the way things were: the hairstyles, clothing, cars, music, etc.

2. Memory book. Yearbooks attempt to tell the story of every person on campus.

Ideally, the yearbook does not represent a particular group of students, but all diverse groups.

3. Reference book. The yearbook provides facts and figures for the year and is reader-friendly with a table of contents, organized sections, and an index.

4. Public relations tool. Yearbooks tell the story of the school. Even a small, rural high school can be made into an exciting place via the yearbook. More and more, yearbooks are being utilized for their P.R. value.

At various times, we look back at these photographic memories with pride, humor, amazement, and, well, embarrassment. Who can resist picking up an old dusty yearbook to flip through the pages? Time stands still for just a moment as you happen upon the forgotten fashions, feared principal, cherished and hated teachers, and autographs and silly writings of long-lost classmates.

Almost everyone can relate to high school, as Ralph Keyes writes in his 1976 book, *Is There Life After High School?*

War is the analogy I keep thinking of to describe how we remember high school. Veterans often tell me they remember their wartime experiences with intense ambivalence: hating the memory and hoping never again to go through combat, while feeling that the constant danger made them alive in a way they sometimes miss. I don't think it's any coincidence that both high school classes and wartime combat units constantly hold reunions. Each group is bonded by a sense of sheer danger. In war, as in high school, friendships are forged that have special depth; love affairs become particularly poignant.

Over the years, many, many former Texas high school students have gone on to distinguish themselves in their chosen professions. If you attended a high school in the Lone Star State, you may have very well been a classmate of a Texas high school hotshot.

Perhaps no other state has produced such a large and diverse group of celebrities, ranging from presidents to athletes to entertainers to, yes, criminals. LBJ, George W. Bush, Shaquille O'Neal, Vanilla Ice, Meat Loaf, Lee Harvey Oswald, and J.R. Ewing —

believe it or not, at one time or another, they all sat in a classroom in Texas.

Texas High School Hotshots is intended to serve as a history book that is not only informative, but one that is both fun and entertaining. The book profiles some 200 hotshots, representing more than 130 high schools, from Abbott to Wink.

It should be pointed out that not all the hotshots graduated. Years ago it was not uncommon for students to drop out of school to enter the military or seek employment to assist their families. (Note: On the school-by-school picture pages, the year listed designates when the hotshot graduated. If no year is listed, the hotshot did not graduate from that school or in a few cases, a graduation date was unavailable.)

In addition to the hotshots listed in each chapter, mention is made of celebrities who were born in Texas and/or who may have attended elementary or junior high school in the state before dropping out or moving. Included in each chapter are "high school confidential" notes — bits of trivia about Texas high school hotshots.

Hotshots also offers a list of famous Texas high school celebrities and the school activities they were involved in and any awards/honors they received. An added bonus throughout the book are actual pages taken from various yearbooks.

Because of space and time constraints, it was impossible to include everyone worthy of consideration in this book. But this is a representative group of both individuals and schools.

And who knows? As history shows, your second grader could one day be a president or governor or rock star. And then it would be time for *Texas High School Hotshots II*.

Yearbook Workers

- H. Ross Perot, Texarkana Texas High (yearbook business manager)
- Horton Foote, Wharton High
- Charles "Tex" Watson, Farmersville High (sports editor)
- Walter Cronkite, Houston San Jacinto High (co-sports editor)
- Jim Lehrer, San Antonio Jefferson High (sports editor)
- Roy Orbison, Wink High
- Ronnie Dunn, Port Isabel High
- Regina Taylor, Dallas Pinkston High
- Sandra Day (O'Connor), El Paso Austin High

Through the Year(books)

Key dates in the evolution of the yearbook:

1845: The first high school yearbook is published in Waterville, N.Y., and is called "The Evergreen."

Mid-1800s: Posed photos and engraved illustrations appear but are expensive. Most books only feature the seniors or graduating class.

1880: The modern yearbook is born. The letterpress process and halftone printing allow for affordable, mass-produced books.

1920: High school yearbooks include school activities and teachers and are not just for seniors anymore.

1925: Schools introduce yearbook sales campaigns.

1930: Offset printing allows photos of all sizes and more affordability. Smaller schools now have yearbooks. Yearbook companies send representatives to schools for sales.

1935: The average yearbook is published for $6.

1940s: Yearbook staffs get more creative with art and design; books are more sophisticated.

1950s: Yearbooks are now used for education, public relations, and student expression.

1960s: Large, dominant photos and two-page spreads are popular due to *Look* and *Life* magazines.

1970s: Experimental books come along. Examples are unbound books in a box, some covered with Levi jeans, and one fashioned like Crayola crayons.

1980s: Beginning of the video yearbook.

1986: Schools begin using computers and desktop publishing to make their own yearbooks.

1990s: Books take a stronger journalistic style, covering news and issues in addition to student life and fun memories.

2000s: CD-ROM books are introduced.

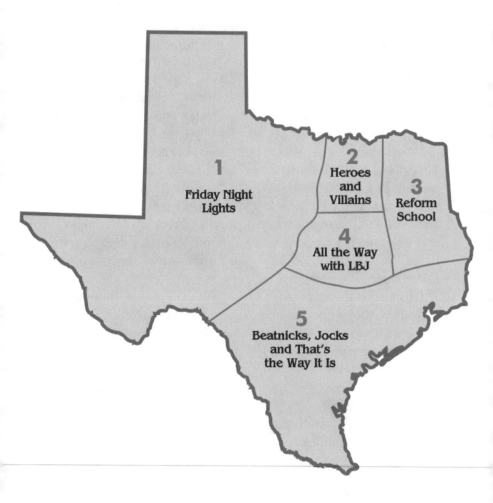

Freshman

West Texas

Friday Night Lights

"I always thought that the best thing to come out of Wink was me and the 1952 state championship football team."

— Roy Orbison (Wink High School, '54)

San Angelo 1940
Yearbook

FOOTBALL

The unclassified Bobcats rose to high rating early in the season by starting the pre-conference games with triumphs over Brownwood, Cisco, Paschal of Ft. Worth, and Brackenridge of San Antonio.

But the Sweetwater Mustangs proved themselves a harder playing ball club when they beat the Bobcats 7-0. The Bobcats did not recover from this defeat until the latter part of the season, when they took victories over Lamesa 7-6, and Abilene 13-9.

The Cats with an unusual scoring attack of passes and hard driving, ability of team work, and a powerful spirit of determination, went to four victories; while the rugged and battering defense held the losing scores close and ended the season with the total points equivalent to 119 for the Bobcats against 94 for the opponents.

The Kittens who took the bumps and knocks to build up a stronger Bobcat team this year will play the Bobcat games next fall.

- - KITTEN LETTERMEN -

John Cargile	Bill Humlong	R. L. McKinney
R. T. Cope	Weldon Kelly	Morty Mertz
Martin Dehnel	Frank Kreidel	Delora Morris
Floyd Dodson	Charles Leonard	F. E. Parker
Alton Edwards	Bobby Lonon	Archie Joe Thurman
Lawrence Guthals	Lee Roy Lyons	Cecil Turner
	Roy McElhaney	

- - BOBCAT MANAGERS -

Douglas Guenthner	Melvin Miller	A. R. Patton	Jack Wilkerson

San Angelo Bobcats 1939

Just a few miles down the road from Wink stands perhaps the most well known high school in the entire state of Texas — Odessa Permian, a school that has been in existence since 1959.

Well known not because of any particular graduates, but because of a visit from a young eastern writer.

In 1988 H. G. "Buzz" Bissinger left his job as a Philadelphia newspaper editor to move to Odessa. During that year, Bissinger "lived with" the legendary Permian football team, attending team meetings, workouts, and games. He interviewed not only players and coaches, but school officials, parents, and townspeople.

His book that followed, *Friday Night Lights*, was a national best seller that spawned controversy throughout West Texas and the nation.

Permian followers were angry and upset, saying that Bissinger betrayed the town's trust with his less-than-flattering win-at-all-cost portrayal of the football program. Death threats prompted the cancellation of book signings Bissinger had scheduled in the area.

The national media got into the act, with the CBS-TV news program *60 Minutes* even going to Odessa to do a feature on the furor.

When all was said and done, everyone agreed that Odessa was not that much different from any other West Texas community in terms of worshipping its football team.

The controversy eventually died down, Bissinger moved away, and life returned to normal.

Vocabulary

Sock hop — a dance popularized at high schools in the 1950s; dancers danced without shoes in order not to scratch the gymnasium floor

Lubbock High School
Yearbook

VIC of ICT Attends District Convention

Nineteen different trades are engaged in by the 36 members of Vocational Industrial Club of Industrial Co-operative Training, Chapter 95. These students work afternoons and have a business meeting once a week.

Socials included a formal initiation at K. N. Clapp Party House and an Employer-Employee Banquet. Tuesday nights the group played basketball or volleyball in the boys' gym.

Representatives went to a district meet in Amarillo and the state meet at Waco. Lawana Hilburn attended these as club sweetheart.

Officers are, clockwise, Charlene Hadaway, secretary; Buddy Holly, vice-president; and Delton Combs, president. Not pictured are James Hogan, treasurer; Bob Montgomery, reporter; and Don Adams, sergeant-at-arms.

Members are Delton Combs, Buddy Holly, Charlene Hadaway, James Hogan, Bob Montgomery, Don Adams, Sarah Adams, J. C. Alexander, Don Allen, David Bowers, Carolyn Cone, Lawrence Dale, Aubrey Davis, James Fread, Reagan Garrett, Eugene Green, Billy Heston, Lawana Hilburn, Amos Hodge, Henry Housour, George Jones, John Jackson, Wayne Jacobs, Don Ledwig, Bobby Mayfield, Jimmie Oglesby, Beverly Patrick, John A. Petty, James Pritchard, Mary Robertson, Norman Williamson, Frank Wilson, Herbert Wilson, Harold Womack, Eddie Yozbick, and Ray Nall.

Frank Wilson is taking a free shot in the basketball game held every Tuesday night in the boys' gym. Other members of the club participating in the activity are Aubrey Davis, James Fread, and Bobby Mayfield.

Beverly Patrick is explaining to James Fread, Wayne Jacobs, Harold Womack, John A. Petty, and Aubrey Davis, the correct places for the keywords, *skill*, *knowledge*, and *experience*, on the club symbol.

190

The Legend of Mojo

Although Odessa Permian only began playing football in 1959, it didn't take long for the school to become a state power. The Panthers captured their first state crown in 1965 and went on to add titles in 1972, '80, '84, '89, and '91.

Through the years, Mojo magic is a mystique that has carried the team to several improbable come-from-behind victories. By definition, "mojo" is an Anglicized version of the French word "montjoy," which was an early battle cry of French kings. In addition, mojo was a voodoo charm used in the southern United States. The origin of Permian mojo has more than one version, according to *The Secret of Mojo*, a book by Regina Walker McCally:

Version 1: At the 1967 game with Abilene Cooper, some former Permian students attending the game from college had too much to drink. They began yelling for their favorite player, a guy named Joe ("Go-Joe, Go-Joe, Go-Joe," they shouted), and fans around them thought they were shouting "Mo-jo, Mo-jo, Mo-jo."

A second version says that at the same game, the Permian cheerleaders used a Mojo chant for the first time after having learned the cheer the previous summer.

According to McCally's book, whatever Mojo is, it was born at that Abilene Cooper game in 1967, a 28-0 thrashing at the hands of Jack Mildren and company. And Permian coach Gene Mayfield vowed never to let it happen again, so Mojo was born out of defeat.

At the Movies: *The Last Picture Show*

During the fall of 1970, a Hollywood film crew arrived in Archer City, Texas (population 1,722), to shoot a movie entitled *The Last Picture Show*. The motion picture was based on the novel of the same name written by Archer City native Larry McMurtry.

Directed by Peter Bogdanovich, the movie featured such future stars as Cybill Shepherd and Jeff Bridges, along with well-known stars Ben Johnson and Cloris Leachman. The story dealt with growing up and the coming of age in small-town Texas in the 1950s. Townspeople were not pleased at having the "dirty story," which featured considerable sex and vulgar language, filmed in their hometown. To almost everyone's surprise, *The Last Picture Show* was both a critical and commercial success, garnering eight Academy Award nominations. Johnson and Leachman won Oscars for Best Supporting Actor and Actress.

Although McMurtry set the story in Archer City, his book referred to the town and school as Thalia (High School). For the movie, the name was changed to Anarene (High School). Scenes were shot in classrooms at Archer City High School, in the gymnasium, and at the old rodeo grounds, which, at the time, served as the school's football field.

In addition to the previously mentioned cast members, the film featured Texas hotshot John Hillerman as an English teacher and character actor Bill Thurman as the stereotypical overweight, tobacco-spewing coach.

West Texas high schools have produced their share of graduates who went on to make a name for themselves.

Midland Lee High School, an archrival of Permian, saw Laura Welch graduate in 1965. Today she is known as First Lady Laura Bush.

Farther west, Sandra Day graduated from Stephen F. Austin High School ('46) in El Paso at the age of sixteen. She ranked sixth in a class of 153. She now carries the moniker of Supreme Court Justice Sandra Day O'Connor and holds the distinction of being the first female Supreme Court Justice. O'Connor returned to her high school homecoming for the first time in fifty years in 1996.

"I think you just have one 50th high school reunion," Justice O'Connor told the *Austin Pioneer* (the school's student newspaper). "It just seemed to me to be something that I very much wanted to do. I wanted to touch base with my roots, the beginning of my scholastic career, and I was just excited to come back."

Country-rock music legend Roy Orbison came out of tiny Wink High School ('54).

Roy Orbison, center, and the Wink Westerners band.

Meanwhile, Lubbock High graduate ('55) Buddy Holly was in the early stages of a rock 'n' roll career that would be cut tragically short by a fatal plane crash in 1959. Another LHS grad from the 1950s was country singer/actor Mac Davis.

A more recent Lubbock High-ex ('92) is Natalie Maines, the lead singer for the country group The Dixie Chicks.

Archer City High School, located a few miles south of Wichita Falls, was home to Larry McMurtry ('54), a Pulitzer Prize winning author. To date McMurtry has written such epics as *Lonesome Dove* and *The Last Picture Show*.

13

Elvis in Texas

We all remember those days of school assemblies in which we trudged down to the auditorium or gym to hear alleged entertainment and/or interesting speakers. More often than not, the entertainment was an off-key choir and the interesting speaker put us quickly to sleep. But if you attended a Texas high school in the mid-fifties, you may have had the good fortune to see an up-and-coming rock and roller perform at your local high school.

Yes, before he hit the big time, Elvis Presley performed an incredible 106 times (1954-56) in Texas. Elvis loved to play at high schools, performing on one or more occasions at the following high school auditoriums/field houses/stadiums: Odessa, Midland, Breckenridge, Stamford, Seymour, Gaston, Alpine, DeKalb, and Conroe. The concert at Alpine High School was a benefit event for the school's Future Farmers of America program.

Among the many outstanding athletes to attend schools in the region were Sweetwater High's Sammy Baugh ('33), a future pro football hall of famer; Abilene Cooper all-state quarterback Jack Mildren ('68), who would later star at the University of Oklahoma and still later serve as lieutenant governor of that state; Throckmorton High's Bob Lilly, a future hall of fame defensive lineman with the Dallas Cowboys. After completing his junior year at Throckmorton, Lilly moved with his family to Oregon, where he graduated from high school. The Stamford High duo of Charles Coody and Charles Stenholm also made their mark on the playing field.

Coody ('55) was an all-district quarterback and state golf winner under legendary coach Gordon Wood. Coody, who also excelled in basketball, enjoyed a successful career on the pro golf tour, winning the 1971 Masters. Stenholm ('57) lettered in football, basketball, and track and was a member of Wood's 1956 state championship football team. Stenholm has served as a U.S. congressman for many years.

Several other hotshots who were born in West Texas or attended area schools at one time or another:

- President George W. Bush was born in New Haven, Conn., but attended elementary school and junior high in Midland. Later he attended Houston Kinkaid, before graduating from the prestigious Phillips Academy in Andover, Maryland. Also a Phillips alum is H.G. "Buzz" Bissinger, author of *Friday Night Lights*.

- Country singer Tanya Tucker was born in Seminole. As a young child, she and her family moved to Arizona. She attended her freshman year of high school in Henderson, Nevada, before quitting to pursue her career in show business.

- ABC News reporter Sam Donaldson was born in El Paso but graduated from New Mexico Military Institute.

- Mary Francis, later known as actress Debbie Reynolds, was born in El Paso but moved to Burbank, Calif., when she was eight years old.

- Florencia Cardona, later known as singer Vikki Carr, was born in El Paso but grew up in California.

- Soccer sensation Mia Hamm was part of a military family. She was born in Alabama but attended elementary school in Wichita Falls and San Antonio. During the middle of her sophomore year at Wichita Falls Notre Dame High, she moved with her family to Lake Braddock, Virginia. She graduated from high school there.

- Actor Woody Harrelson was born in Midland but grew up and attended school in Lebanon, Ohio.

- Gene Roddenberry, the creator of TV's *Star Trek*, was born in El Paso. He grew up in Los Angeles.

15

- Actress/dancer Cyd Charisse was born Tula Ellice Finklea in Amarillo in 1921. She left the state as a teenager to begin her career.
- Western swing king Bob Wills was born in tiny Kosse in West Texas in 1905. His education ended after the seventh grade at Friendship School.
- Actress Judith Ivey was born in El Paso and later lived in Big Spring and Odessa. At age ten she and her family moved to Michigan.
- In 1944 Jimmy Dean dropped out of Plainview High School to join the merchant marines. Dean later gained fame as a country music entertainer and as the head of a successful sausage business.
- Folksinger Woody Guthrie was born in Okemah, Oklahoma. He moved to Pampa, Texas in 1929. After an undistinguished academic career, he dropped out of Pampa High in the early 1930s.
- Famed jockey Willie Shoemaker was born in Fabens, Texas (near El Paso), but at age 8, moved with his family to El Monte, California, where he completed high school.

Jocks

- Patrick Swayze, Houston Waltrip (football, track, diving)
- Nolan Ryan, Alvin (baseball, basketball)
- Lyndon B. Johnson, Johnson City (baseball)
- John Denver, Fort Worth Arlington Heights (football)
- Boz Scaggs, St. Mark's (soccer, track and field)
- Steve Miller, Dallas Woodrow Wilson (football, track and field)
- J. P. Richardson Jr., Beaumont (football, tennis)
- B. J. Thomas, Lamar Consolidated (baseball)

- Marvin Lee Aday (Meat Loaf), Dallas Thomas Jefferson (football, baseball, track)
- Don Baylor, Austin Stephen F. Austin (baseball, football, basketball)
- Ben Crenshaw, Austin Stephen F. Austin (golf)
- Tom Kite, Austin McCallum (golf)
- Mike Hargrove, Perryton (football)
- Dan Rather, Houston Reagan (football)
- Larry Gatlin, Odessa High (football)
- Willie Nelson, Abbott High (football)
- Babe Didrikson Zaharias, Beaumont (volleyball, tennis, golf, baseball, swimming, basketball)
- Woodard "Tex" Ritter, Beaumont South Park (basketball, football, baseball)
- William P. Clements Jr., Highland Park (football)
- Ernie Banks, Dallas Booker T. Washington (baseball, football, track, basketball)
- Charles "Tex" Watson, Farmersville (football, basketball, track)
- Michael Johnson, Dallas Skyline (track)
- Larry Johnson, Dallas Skyline (basketball)
- Joe Don Looney, Fort Worth Paschal (football, track)
- Brian Bosworth, Irving MacArthur (football, basketball)
- Kent Waldrep, Alvin (football)
- Tom Landry, Mission (football, basketball, track)
- Dr. Denton Cooley, Houston San Jacinto (basketball)
- Justin Leonard, Richardson Lake Highlands (golf)
- Norm Cash, Post (football)
- Roger Clemens, Houston Spring Woods (baseball, football)
- Jim Reeves, Carthage (baseball)
- Steve Austin, Edna (football)
- John Mahaffey, Kerrville Tivy (golf, basketball, football)
- Charles Coody, Stamford (golf, football, basketball)
- Walter Cronkite, Houston San Jacinto (track)
- George W. Bush, Houston Kinkaid (baseball)

17

- Fess Parker, San Angelo (football)
- Jack Mildren, Abilene Cooper (football, track, basketball)
- Matthew McConaughey, Longview (tennis, golf)
- Jamie Foxx, Terrell (football, track)
- G. A. Moore Jr., Pilot Point (football, basketball, track, baseball)
- Joe Don Baker, Groesbeck (football)
- Karen Parfitt Hughes, Dallas W. T. White (swimming)
- Bobby Layne, Highland Park (football, basketball, baseball)
- Doak Walker, Highland Park (football, basketball, baseball, track, swimming)
- Andre Ware, Dickinson (football, basketball, baseball, track)
- Drayton McLane, Cameron Yoe (tennis, softball, basketball)
- Bob Bullock, Hillsboro (football, track, basketball manager)
- Tracy Scoggins, Dickinson (tennis)
- Mia Hamm, Wichita Falls Notre Dame (soccer)
- Gordon Wood, Abilene Wylie (basketball, track)
- Rick Perry, Paint Creek (football, basketball, track)
- Forrest Gregg, Sulphur Springs (football, basketball, baseball)
- Johnny Lee, Santa Fe (baseball)
- Walt Garrison, Lewisville (football, baseball, track, basketball)
- Randy Matson, Pampa (track, basketball, football)
- Rogers Hornsby, Fort Worth North Side (baseball, football)
- Charles Stenholm, Stamford (football, basketball, track)
- Davey O'Brien, Dallas Woodrow Wilson (football, basketball, baseball, track)
- Gene Stallings, Paris (football, basketball, golf)
- Forrest "Blackie" Sherrod, Belton (football, basketball, track)

Abilene Cooper High

JACK MILDREN
(1968)
Oklahoma Sooners
quarterback
Oklahoma Lieutenant
Governor

Abilene Wylie High

GORDON WOOD
(1934)
Legendary Texas high
school football coach

Anson High

JEANNIE CAROLYN
STEPHENSON
(1964)

JEANNIE C. RILEY
Pop singer, "Harper
Valley PTA"

19

Archer City High

LARRY McMURTRY
(1954)
Pulitzer Prize winning
author
*Lonesome Dove,
The Last Picture Show*

Brownfield High

SHERYL SWOOPES
(1989)
Pro basketball player

El Paso Stephen F. Austin High

SANDRA DAY
(1946)

SANDRA DAY
O'CONNOR
United States Supreme
Court Justice

Fort Stockton High

CLAYTON WILLIAMS
(1950)
Oilman/gubernatorial
candidate

Tom S. Lubbock High

BUDDY HOLLEY
(1955)

BUDDY HOLLY
Rock 'n' Roll music
pioneer

Tom S. Lubbock High

MAC DAVIS
(1960)
Singer/actor

Tom S. Lubbock High

NATALIE MAINES
(1992)
Country musician
The Dixie Chicks

Lubbock Monterey High

LEONARD CORBIN
(1958)

BARRY CORBIN
Actor
Northern Exposure

Midland Robert E. Lee High

LAURA WELCH
(1965)

LAURA BUSH
First Lady

Odessa High

HAYDEN FRY
(1946)
College football coach

Odessa High

LARRY GATLIN
(1966)
Country musician

Paint Creek School

RICK PERRY
(1969)
Governor of Texas

Pampa High

RANDY MATSON
(1963)
Olympic shot-putter

Perryton High

MIKE HARGROVE
(1968)
Major league baseball
player/manager

Plainview High

JIMMY DEAN
Country
entertainer/businessman

Post High

NORM CASH
(1951)
Major league baseball
player

San Angelo Central High

F. E. PARKER
(1942)

FESS PARKER
Actor
Davy Crockett,
Daniel Boone

High School Confidential

While a fourth grader at Sam Houston Elementary School in Midland, young George W. Bush was sent to the principal's office. His offense? Creating a distur-bance by marking up his face with a ballpoint pen (sideburns, etc.) to resemble Elvis Presley.

25

Snyder High

POWERS BOOTHE
(1967)
Actor
*Guyana Tragedy: The Story
of Jim Jones*

Stamford High

CHARLES COODY
(1955)
Pro golfer, Masters
champion

Stamford High

CHARLES STENHOLM
(1957)
U.S. congressman

Stephenville High

LEE ROY PARNELL
(1975)
Country musician

Stinnett High (Now West Texas High)

DONNY ANDERSON
(1961)
Pro football player

Sweetwater High

SAMMY BAUGH
(1933)
Hall of Fame pro
quarterback

Throckmorton High

BOB LILLY
Hall of Fame pro football
player
Dallas Cowboys

Wichita Falls Notre Dame

MIA HAMM
Olympic soccer player

Wink High

ROY ORBISON
(1954)
Rock 'n' Roll music
pioneer

Not Pictured:

Littlefield High
WAYLON JENNINGS
Country musician

Midland High
LARRY L. KING
(1946)
Author, *Best Little Whorehouse in Texas*

O'Donnell High
DAN BLOCKER
(1946)
TV actor, *Bonanza*

THE PLAINVIEW '44

PLAINVIEW HIGH SCHOOL

Jocks Candids

Abilene Cooper quarterback Jack Mildren avoids the tackle of a Midland Lee player. Mildren became a wishbone quarterback at the University of Oklahoma and was later elected lieutenant governor of Oklahoma.

Left to right are Paris Wildcat standouts in 1949: Raymond Berry, Sammy Morrow, Billy Alexander.

The 1949 Paris Wildcat football team.

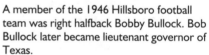

A member of the 1946 Hillsboro football team was right halfback Bobby Bullock. Bob Bullock later became lieutenant governor of Texas.

Dickinson High School quarterback Andre Ware takes a break on the sidelines. While quarterbacking the Houston Cougars, Ware won the Heisman Trophy in 1989.

Walt Garrison was a hard-running fullback for the Lewisville Fighting Farmers. After playing collegiately at Oklahoma State, Garrison was a member of the Dallas Cowboys.

Farmersville High School all-district halfback Charles Watson.

Charles "Tex" Watson breaks loose for a touchdown run for the Farmersville Farmers in 1963. In the late sixties, Watson joined the notorious Manson family in California. He is serving a life prison sentence for his involvement in the Tate-LaBianca murders.

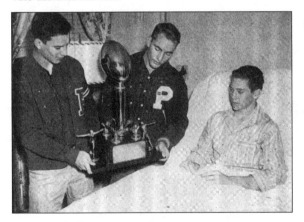

John Deutschendorf of the Fort Worth Arlington Heights Yellowjackets. After changing his name to John Denver, he became an international star in the 1970s as a pop singer.

Paris Wildcat receiver Raymond Berry rests in the hospital after being injured in a game against Greenville in 1949. Cheering him up by holding the district championship trophy are teammates Sammy Morrow and Bobby Buckman.

A team picture of the 1952 Sulphur Springs Wildcat basketball team. Shown on the back row, third from left, is Forrest Gregg, who would become a star football player in the National Football League.

Sulphur Springs center Forrest Gregg shows his form.

Dickinson Gator Andre Ware jumps high for a rebound in this 1985 game against Clear Creek.

Gene Stallings, a member of the Paris Wildcat basketball team, circa 1950.

Larry Johnson

ON TOP OF IT ALL

Ever since Larry Johnson showed up on the basketball scene as a freshman, he's been in the media limelight. Making the varsity as a freshman was his first accomplishment but he's made many since then.

While others referred to Johnson as a star, he didn't see himself that way. "I'm not the star of the team. There are eight more people on the team doing the same things that I do," said Johnson.

Johnson saw the sport a little differently than some. "I feel that basketball shouldn't be played as a job. When basketball is played as a job, it puts too much strain on you. It should be played for the fun."

Whether Johnson saw it as fun or not, others have recognized his obvious talent. He's received over 100 letters from colleges expressing interest in him. While he was too young to be contacted in person by the scouts, that didn't keep him from thinking about his future.

"I'd like to go to a college where the games are televised," said Johnson. He also wanted to go someplace where he would be able to play as a freshman. Georgetown was his first choice.

Johnson looked up to a number of people.

He credited his seventh grade coach, Edward Wesley, with helping him and seniors on the team for much encouragement.

Still, the pros was where Johnson looked for his idols. Michael Jordan and Patrick Ewing were the first names to come to his mind. "I would like to be like Michael Jordan because he's the best," said Johnson.

After college and a career in the pros, Johnson doesn't plan to rest on his laurels. He plans to become a business man and his own recreation center or a small gymnasium.

—Angela Vicks

Spring Woods High School pitcher Roger Clemens fires a pitch during a 1979 game. After an outstanding career at the University of Texas, Clemens starred in the major leagues, winning the Cy Young Award.

Don Baylor of Austin Stephen F. Austin High prepares to swing during this 1966 game. Baylor enjoyed an outstanding career with the Baltimore Orioles and also managed in the big leagues.

35

B. J. Thomas played third base for Rosenberg Lamar Consolidated High School in the late 1950s. Thomas scored big on the pop charts with such 1970s hits as "Raindrops Keep Falling on My Head" and "Hooked on a Feeling."

The 1962 Lewisville Farmer baseball team. Standing third from the left is future Dallas Cowboys football star Walt Garrison.

Jack Mildren runs the mile for the Abilene Cooper Cougars. Mildren excelled in football at the University of Oklahoma and later was elected to public office in the Sooner State.

Steve Miller throws the discus as a member of the Dallas Woodrow Wilson track team in 1961. While leading the Steve Miller Band, he produced such rock/pop hit songs as "The Joker," "Take the Money and Run," and "Abracadabra."

Future U.S. Open Champion Tom Kite works on his swing while a student at Austin McCallum in the 1960s.

Ben Crenshaw practices his swing as a member of the Austin Stephen F. Austin golf team in the late 1960s. "Gentle Ben" went on to become a two-time Masters champion.

A team photo of the Dallas W. T. White girls' swim team in 1970. Shown on the front row, sixth from the left, is Karen Parfitt. Karen Parfitt Hughes served as an advisor to President George W. Bush.

A member of the Dickinson High girls' tennis team was future actress Tracy Scoggins, standing center.

Bill Scaggs was a standout soccer player at St. Mark's School of Texas in the 1960s. Boz Scaggs was a standout rock/pop performer in the 1970s, winning a Grammy for his 1976 album *Silk Degrees*.

Guy Lewis as a quarterback at Arp.

Future pro football hall of famer Kyle Rote was a standout athlete at San Antonio Thomas Jefferson High School in the 1940s.

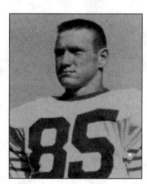

Another standout athlete at San Antonio Jefferson was linebacker Tommy Nobis (1960s).

Guy Lewis made a name for himself as the basketball coach at the University of Houston. He participated in several sports at Arp High School.

Texas High School Football State Champions

(Year-by-year; UIL-University Interscholastic League, PVIL-Prairie View Interscholastic League)

1920—Houston Heights, Cleburne
1921—Bryan
1922—Waco
1923—Abilene
1924—Oak Cliff
1925—Waco
1926—Waco
1927—Waco
1928—Abilene
1929—Port Arthur, Breckenridge
1930—Tyler
1931—Abilene
1932—Corsicana, Masonic Home
1933—Greenville
1934—Amarillo
1935—Amarillo
1936—Amarillo
1937—Longview
1938—Corpus Christi
1939—Lubbock
1940—UIL—Amarillo
    PVIL 2A—Ft. Worth Terrell
1941—UIL—Wichita Falls
    PVIL 2A—Dallas Washington
1942—UIL—Austin
    PVIL 2A—Austin Anderson
1943—UIL—San Angelo
    PVIL 2A—Wichita Falls
    Washington, Houston Yates

1944—UIL—Port Arthur
    PVIL 2A—Houston Wheatley
1945—UIL—Highland Park, Waco
    PVIL 2A—Wichita Falls
    Washington
1946—UIL—Odessa
    PVIL 2A—Dallas Washington,
    Galveston Central
1947—UIL—San Angelo Breckenridge
    PVIL 2A—Ft. Worth Terrell
    PVIL A—Denison Terrell,
    Taylor
1948—UIL City—Ft. Worth Arlington
    Heights
    UIL 2A—Waco
    UIL A—Monahans
    PVIL 2A—Corpus Christi Coles
    PVIL A—Denison Terrell
1949—UIL City—San Antonio Jefferson
    UIL 2A—Wichita Falls
    UIL A—Littlefield
    PVIL 2A—Dallas Lincoln
    PVIL A—Orange Wallace
1950—UIL City—Dallas Sunset
    UIL 2A—Wichita Falls
    UIL A—Wharton
    PVIL 2A—Dallas Washington
    PVIL A—San Angelo Blackshear
1951—UIL 4A—Lubbock

UIL 3A—Breckenridge
UIL 2A—Arlington
UIL A—Giddings
PVIL 2A—Houston Yates, Waco Moore
PVIL A—Huntsville Sam Houston
1952—UIL 4A—Lubbock
UIL 3A—Breckenridge
UIL 2A—Terrell
UIL A—Wink
PVIL 3A—Waco Moore
PVIL 2A—Amarillo Carver
PVIL A—Arp Industrial
1953—UIL 4A—Houston Lamar
UIL 3A—Port Neches
UIL 2A—Huntsville
UIL A—Ranger
PVIL 3A—Port Arthur Lincoln
PVIL 2A—Corsicana Jackson
PVIL A—Livingston Dunbar
1954—UIL 4A—Abilene
UIL 3A—Breckenridge
UIL 2A—Phillips
UIL A—Deer Park
PVIL 3A—Houston Wheatley
PVIL 2A—Orange Wallace
PVIL A—Livingston Dunbar
1955—UIL 4A—Abilene
UIL 3A—Port Neches
UIL 2A—Stamford
UIL A—Deer Park, Stinnett
PVIL 3A—Port Arthur Lincoln
PVIL 2A—Baytown Carver
PVIL A—Rockdale Aycock
1956—UIL 4A—Abilene
UIL 3A—Garland
UIL 2A—Stamford
UIL A—Stinnett

PVIL 3A—Austin Anderson
PVIL 2A—Corsicana Jackson
PVIL A—Sealy Cnty Austin
1957—UIL 4A—Highland Park
UIL 3A—Nederland
UIL 2A—Terrell
UIL A—Mart, White Oak
PVIL 3A—Austin Anderson
PVIL 2A—Corsicana Jackson
PVIL A—Galena Park Fidelity Manor
1958—UIL 4A—Wichita Falls
UIL 3A—Breckenridge
UIL 2A—Stamford
UIL A—White Deer
PVIL 3A—Dallas Washington
PVIL 2A—Baytown Carver
PVIL A—Livingston Dunbar
1959—UIL 4A—Corpus Christi Ray
UIL 3A—Breckenridge, Cleburne
UIL 2A—Stamford
UIL A—Katy
PVIL 3A—Beaumont Hebert
PVIL 2A—Bay City Hilliard
PVIL A—West Dunbar
1960—UIL 4A—Corpus Christi Miller
UIL 3A—Brownwood
UIL 2A—Denver City
UIL A—Albany
PVIL 4A—Houston Washington, Waco Moore
PVIL 3A—Corpus Christi Coles
PVIL 2A—Conroe Washington
PVIL A—Freeport Lanier
1961—UIL 4A—Wichita Falls
UIL 3A—Dumas
UIL 2A—Donna
UIL A—Albany

PVIL 4A—Austin Anderson
PVIL 3A—Baytown Carver
PVIL 2A—Midland Carver
PVIL A—Richardson Hamilton
Park
1962—UIL 4A—San Antonio
Brackenridge
UIL 3A—Dumas
UIL 2A—Jacksboro
UIL A—Rotan
PVIL 4A—Houston Yates
PVIL 3A—Ft. Worth Kirkpatrick
PVIL 2A—Wharton Training
PVIL A—Taylor Price
1963—UIL 4A—Garland
UIL 3A—Corsicana
UIL 2A—Rockwall
UIL A—Petersburg
PVIL 4A—Galveston Central
PVIL 3A—Ft. Worth Kirkpatrick
PVIL 2A—Lubbock Dunbar
PVIL A—Smithville Brown
1964—UIL 4A—Garland
UIL 3A—Palestine
UIL 2A—Palacios
UIL A—Archer City
PVIL 4A—Waco Moore
PVIL 3A—Lufkin Dunbar
PVIL 2A—Sherman Douglass
PVIL A—Bartlett Washington
1965—UIL 4A—Odessa Permian
UIL 3A—Brownwood
UIL 2A—Plano
UIL A—Wills Point
PVIL 4A—Houston Yates
PVIL 3A—Wichita Falls
Washington
PVIL 2A—Conroe Washington
PVIL A—Sweeny

1966—UIL 4A—San Angelo
UIL 3A—Bridge City
UIL 2A—Sweeny
UIL A—Sonora
PVIL 4A—Beaumont Hebert
PVIL 3A—Lufkin Dunbar
PVIL 2A—Bay City Hilliard
1967—UIL 4A—Austin Reagan
UIL 3A—Brownwood
UIL 2A—Plano
UIL A—Tidehaven
PVIL 3A—Lufkin Dunbar
PVIL 2A—Jasper Rowe
1968—UIL 4A—Austin Reagan
UIL 3A—Lubbock Estacado
UIL 2A—Daingerfield
UIL A—Sonora
PVIL 3A—Corsicana Jackson
1969—UIL 4A—Wichita Falls
UIL 3A—Brownwood
UIL 2A—Iowa Park
UIL A—Mart
PVIL 3A—Weirgate
1970—4A—Austin Reagan
3A—Brownwood
2A—Refugio, Iowa Park
A—Sonora
1971—4A—San Antonio Lee
3A—Plano
2A—Jacksboro
A—Barbers Hill, Sonora
1972—4A—Odessa Permian
3A—Uvalde
2A—Bowling
A—Schulenburg
B—Chilton
8-man—Goree
6-man—O'Brien
1973—4A—Tyler

41

3A—Cuero
2A—Friendswood
A—Troup
B—Big Sandy
8-man—Goree
6-man—Cherokee
1974—4A—Brazoswood
3A—Cuero
2A—Newton
A—Grapeland
B—Big Sandy, Celina
8-man—Follett
6-man—Marathon
1975—4A—Port Neches
3A—Ennis
2A—LaGrange
A—DeLeon
B—Big Sandy
8-man—Leakey
6-man—Cherokee
1976—4A—San Antonio Churchill
3A—Beaumont Hebert
2A—Rockdale
A—Barbers Hill
B—Gorman
6-man—Marathon
1977—4A—Plano
3A—Dickinson
2A—Wylie
A—Bernard
B—Wheeler
6-man—May
1978—4A—Houston Stratford
3A—Brownwood
2A—Sealy
A—China Springs
B—Union Hill
6-man—Cherokee
1979—4A—Temple

3A—McKinney
2A—Van
A—Hull-Daisetta
B—Wheeler
6-man—Milford
1980—5A—Odessa Permian
4A—Huntsville
3A—Pittsburg
2A—Pilot Point, Tidehaven
A—Valley View
6-man—Milford
1981—5A—Lake Highlands
4A—Brownwood
3A—Cameron
2A—Pilot Point
A—Bremond
6-man—Whitharral
1982—5A—Beaumont West Brook
4A—Willowridge
3A—Refugio
2A—Eastland
A—Union Hill
6-man—Highland
1983—5A—Converse Judson
4A—Bay City
3A—Daingerfield
2A—Boyd
A—Knox City
6-man—Highland
1984—5A—Odessa Permian,
Beaumont French
4A—Denison
3A—Medina Valley
2A—Groveton
A—Munday
6-man—Jayton
1985—5A—Houston Yates
4A—Sweetwater
3A—Daingerfield

2A—Electra
A—Goldthwaite
6-man—Jayton
1986—5A—Plano
4A—West Orange-Stark
3A—Jefferson
2A—Shiner
A—Burkeville
6-man—Fort Hancock
1987—5A—Plano
4A—West Orange-Stark
3A—Cuero
2A—Lorena
A—Wheeler
6-man—Lohn
1988—5A—Dallas Carter
4A—Paris
3A—Southlake Carroll
2A—Corrigan-Camden
A—White Deer
6-man—Fort Hancock
1989—5A—Odessa Permian
4A—Tyler Chapel Hill
3A—Mexia
2A—Groveton
A—Thorndale
6-man—Fort Hancock
1990—5A BS—Marshall
5A RS—Aldine
4A—Wilmer-Hutchins
3A—Vernon
2A—Groveton
A—Bartlett
6-man—Fort Hancock
1991—5A DI—Killeen
5A DII—Odessa Permian
4A—A & M Consolidated
3A—Groesbeck
2A—Schulenburg

A—Memphis
6-man—Fort Hancock
1992—5A DI—Converse Judson
5A DII—Temple
4A—Waxahachie
3A—Southlake Carroll
2A—Schulenburg
A—Bartlett
6-man—Panther Creek
1993—5A DI—Converse Judson
5A DII—Lewisville
4A—Stephenville
3A—Southlake Carroll
2A—Goldthwaite
A—Sudan
6-man—Panther Creek
1994—5A DI—Plano
5A DII—Tyler John Tyler
4A—Stephenville
3A—Sealy
2A—Goldthwaite
A—Thorndale
6-man—Amherst
1995—5A DI—Converse Judson
5A DII—San Antonio Roosevelt
4A—LaMarque
3A—Sealy
2A—Celina
A—Thorndale
6-man—Amherst
1996—5A DI—Lewisville
5A DII—Austin Westlake
4A DI—Grapevine
4A DII—LaMarque
3A—Sealy
2A—Iraan
A—Windthorst
6-man—Gordon
1997—5A DI—Katy

5A DII—Flower Mound Marcus
4A DI—Texas City
4A DII—LaMarque
3A—Sealy
2A—Stanton
A—Granger
6-man—Borden County
1998—5A DI—Duncanville
5A DII—Midland Lee
4A DI—Grapevine
4A DII—Stephenville
3A DI—Aledo
3A DII—Newton
2A DI—Omaha Paul Pewitt
2A DII—Celina
A—Tenaha
6-man—Trinidad
1999—5A DI—Midland Lee
5A DII—Garland
4A DI—Texas City
4A DII—Stephenville
3A DI—Liberty Eylau
3A DII—Commerce
2A DI—Mart

2A DII—Celina
A—Bartlett
6-man—Gordon
2000—5A DI—Midland Lee
5A DII—Katy
4A DI—Bay City
4A DII—Ennis
3A D1—Gatesville
3A D2—LaGrange
2A D1—Sonora
2A DII—Celina
A—Stratford
6-man—Panther Creek
2001—5A DI—Mesquite
5A DII—Lufkin
4A DI—Denton Ryan
4A DII—Ennis
3A DI—Everman
3A DII—Commerce
2A DI—Blanco
2A DII—Celina
A—Burkeville
6-man—Whitharral

Sophomore

North Texas

Heroes and Villains

"There's lots better things to be in this world than some football player. Doctors, scientists, diplomats. But if they grew up in Texas, who'd they get to take to the dance? They weren't nothing in high school, were they?"

— Mike Renfro, Fort Worth Arlington Heights ('74), college and pro football player

Lewisville High School Yearbook

School Song

Far down in a town so noble,

Challenging the eye,

Stands a school above all others,

Stands our Lewisville High.

Lewisville High, to thee we shall be,

Ever loyal and true,

Fighting always to do service,

For Maroon and White.

North Texas high schools have produced more "heroes and villains" than any other region of the state.

Among the heroes emerging from area schools include a governor, three Heisman Trophy winners, two Miss Americas, an Olympic track star, and a Hall of Fame baseball player.

Among the villains emerging from North Texas schools were two accused presidential assassins, a member of the notorious Manson family, a cult leader, a mass murderer, and TV's greatest villain.

*****

In 1978 William P. Clements Jr. (Highland Park '34), became the first Republican governor in Texas since Reconstruction. Clements served two terms (not consecutive) as governor.

At Highland Park High School, located in an affluent section of north Dallas, Clements made quite a name for himself. He was elected class president three years in a row and was also the first football player from the school to be selected to the all-state team.

Clements is not the only famous name to attend HPHS. Starring on the gridiron for the Scots in the 1940s were Bobby Layne ('44) and Doak Walker ('45), with the latter winning the Heisman Trophy while playing for Southern Methodist University in 1948.

A 1973 graduate of Highland Park is John Hinckley Jr., the man whose gunshots wounded President Ronald Reagan.

And speaking of the Heisman Trophy — it is college football's most prestigious award. The Heisman has been presented annually (since 1935) to the nation's outstanding player by the Downtown Athletic Club of New York City.

Through the years, only one public high school in the country has produced two Heisman Trophy winners — Woodrow Wilson High School of Dallas.

Quarterback Davey O'Brien ('35), who played collegiately at Texas Christian University, won the coveted award in 1938; nearly 50 years later, Woodrow graduate and Notre Dame wide receiver Tim Brown ('84) took home the award. In addition to the two Heisman Trophy winners, Woodrow produced a championship pro golfer in Ralph Guldahl ('30). Guldahl won the U.S. Open in back-to-back years (1937-38) and captured the Masters in 1939.

Jerry Haynes, a 1944 Woodrow graduate, enjoyed a successful career in television. Haynes is best known for his role as Mr. Peppermint on a Dallas station's children's show in the 1960s.

Another Woodrow grad is musician Steve Miller ('61), whose Steve Miller Band produced numerous hit records in the 1970s. It should be noted that Miller completed his last year of studies at Woodrow after being kicked out of Dallas' exclusive St. Mark's School of Texas. A classmate of Miller's at St. Mark's was William "Boz" Scaggs. The two played in a band together (The Marksmen) while in school. They drifted apart, then briefly rejoined for the Steve Miller Band in the late 1960s. Scaggs then went solo, producing a number of hits during the 1970s disco era.

In 1983 Scaggs and Miller returned to St. Mark's and revived The Marksmen in observance of the school's 50th anniversary. At that reunion, Miller offered these sentiments to *The Dallas Morning News*: "Well, let's see. They kicked me out my junior year, in 1960. Being in a rock band and all, I guess they thought we were a little unruly. There were only 32 in the class and they kicked out eight of us…But listen, man, it's great to be back. All my friends are here."

Other notable graduates of St. Mark's include actor Tommy Lee Jones ('65) and businessman Ross Perot Jr.

What Woodrow Wilson is to the Heisman Trophy, Denton High is to the Miss America beauty pageant. Denton High has produced not one but two Miss America winners. Perhaps the school's most famous grad is Phyllis George ('67). She was Miss America of 1971 and later was one of the first female sportscasters on national television. For many years she was married to Kentucky Gov. John Y. Brown.

Shirley Cothran, a 1973 DHS grad, was Miss America in 1975.

Dallas Skyline High School has seen two world-class athletes walk through its corridors. As a matter of fact, Olympic sprinter Michael Johnson ('86) and NBA basketball star Larry Johnson ('87) were classmates at Skyline.

Michael Johnson

After attending Dallas public schools in grades 5-8, Richard Speck enrolled in Dallas Crozier Technical High in the fall of 1957. He flunked physical education, earned no credits, and did not return for the next semester. In 1966 Speck murdered eight student nurses in Chicago in one of America's worst-ever crimes.

In the early 1920s, a young girl by the name of Bonnie Parker attended Dallas Bryan Street High School. (Dallas Bryan Street High School was later known as Dallas Technical High School. In 1942, the name was changed to Crozier Tech.) She was an outstanding student and won a citywide spelling bee. Parker would later be a member of the notorious Bonnie and Clyde outlaw gang. (Her partner in crime, Clyde Barrow, was enrolled in the sixth grade at Sidney Lanier Elementary School in Dallas but quit after one week of classes.)

Meanwhile, over in Fort Worth, a number of famous and infamous people have attended Arlington Heights High School.

Lee Harvey Oswald, the accused assassin of President John F. Kennedy, attended elementary school in Fort Worth before moving to New York and, later, New Orleans. Oswald returned to Fort Worth in 1956. He enrolled as a sophomore that fall at Arlington Heights. On September 28, 1956, he dropped out; he joined the Marines the next month.

Another controversial figure attending AHHS was T. Cullen Davis ('51). In the 1970s, the millionaire businessman was accused of a grisly murder at his Fort Worth mansion.

Defended by Houston lawyer Richard "Racehorse" Haynes (Houston Reagan High), Davis would win acquittal.

What's in a Name?

Sorry to squash the rumor, music fans, but Bryan Adams High School in Dallas is not named in honor of rock singer Bryan Adams.

Adams, who was born in Kingston, Canada in 1959, burts onto the music scene in the 1980s. His hit singles include, "(Everything I Do) I Do It For You," "Heaven," "All For Love," "Have You Ever Really Loved A Woman?", "Cuts Like A Knife," "Straight From the Heart," and "Summer of '69."

And Bryan Adams High School?

It's named for the Bryan Adams who served as school board secretary/business manager for the DISD from 1943-55. Bryan Adams (the school)

opened its doors for the first time in 1957 — two years before Bryan Adams (the singer) was born.

Two other DISD high schools — Kimball and White — are named in honor of former DISD superintendents. Justin F. Kimball was superintendent from 1914-26; Warren Travis White served in that position from 1945 until the late 1960s. Crozier Technical High School, which is no longer in existence, was named for N. R. Crozier, the Dallas superintendent from 1924-40.

And Dallas Carter High bears the name of former DISD board member Dr. David Carter (1925-50).

Crozier Tech and History

No other high school in Dallas underwent more name changes and held more history than the campus located on Bryan Street in downtown Dallas. It first opened in 1884 as Central High School. In 1908 the name was changed to Dallas High. By 1916 it was known as Main High. From 1917-28 the school carried the name of Bryan High. In 1929 the school became known as Dallas Technical High School. Finally, in 1942, the school was renamed Crozier Technical in honor of longtime Dallas superintendent of schools, N. R. Crozier. The school closed in the late 1960s.

Crozier Tech had its share of highlights over the years. The school was a basketball power, winning state championships in 1946, '48, and '55.

And two Crozier Tech class-mates in the mid-1950s — Trini Lopez and Domingo Samudio — went on to achieve fame in pop music circles. Lopez had four top 40 hits ("If I Had A Ham-mer," "Kansas City," "Lemon Tree," and "I'm Comin' Home") from 1963-66. Lopez dropped out of school in his senior year to help support his family. Meanwhile, Samudio, also known as Sam, was leading Sam the Sham and the Pharoahs on the charts. From 1965-67, the group produced six top 40 songs: "Wooly Bully," "Ju Ju Hand," "Ring Dang Doo," "Li'l Red Riding Hood," "The Hair On My Chinny Chin Chin," and "How Do You Catch A Girl."

****

Another Fort Worth Arlington Heights student was Henry John Deutschendorf ('61). In the 1970s he became a pop superstar under the name John Denver.

And in 1964 tiny Farmers-ville High School (located just east of Dallas in Collin County) graduated 34 seniors. Among those graduates was a young man who was an all-district football player, track standout, and honor student. He would eventually move to California.

In 1969 Farmersville High School graduate Charles "Tex" Watson was introduced to a stunned nation as the chief lieutenant in Charles Manson's hippie cult. Watson and five other members of the Manson Family were later convicted in the Tate-LaBianca murders. (One of the victims, actress Sharon Tate, was born in Dallas and attended schools in Dallas, Houston, and El Paso before graduating from high school in Italy.) Watson, who allegedly did most of the killing, remains in a California prison today, where he is a born-again Christian minister.

Vernon Howell, later known to the world as Branch Davidian cult leader David Koresh, dropped out of high school in Garland in his junior year.

A 1949 graduate of Weatherford High is Larry Hagman, who portrayed the wheeler-dealer businessman J. R. Ewing on the 1980s hit TV show *Dallas*. Hagman's mother was actress/dancer Mary Martin of *Peter Pan* fame, also a WHS alum.

W. H. Adamson High in Dallas has turned out four musicians who achieved fame in country/folk circles: Ray Price ('46), Michael Martin Murphey ('63), Ray Wylie Hubbard ('65), and B. W. Stevenson ('67). The latter three (along with a fourth classmate named Larry Groce, who recorded the top-10 hit "Junk Food Junkie" in 1976) were classmates and played folk music at school assemblies.

Not to be outdone, Dallas Thomas Jefferson High gave the world Brenda Vacarro ('58), Michael Nesmith ('61), and Marvin Lee Aday ('66).

Vacarro, who transferred to TJ from The Hockaday School for Girls, gained prominence as an actress. Nesmith, whose mother (Bette Graham) garnered fame and fortune for inventing Liquid Paper, was a member of the TV-pop music group The Monkees. And Marvin Lee Aday is better known as theatrical rock performer/actor Meat Loaf.

Dennis Rodman ('76), the controversial pro basketball player turned entertainer, is a graduate of South Oak Cliff High School in Dallas.

And the relatively new Booker T. Washington High School for the Visual and Performing Arts in Dallas takes pride in the success of three of its former students in the music world: R&B vocalist Erykah Badu, trumpet player Roy Hargrove Jr., and rock singer Edie Brickell.

Prior to integration, Booker T. Washington was an all-black school. Among the prominent students at this school were future Hall of Fame baseball player Ernie Banks ('49) and future World Welterweight Boxing champion Curtis Cokes, who attended school there in the 1950s.

Four-time Tour de France winner Lance Armstrong was planning on being a 1990 graduate of Plano East Senior High School. But he didn't graduate there because of an excessive amount of unexcused absences. (In his autobiography, *It's Not About the Bike: My Journey Back to Life*, Armstrong notes that he missed six weeks of school during his senior year while competing in Olympic-type cycling competition in Colorado Springs and Moscow.)

Late in his senior year at PESH, Armstrong transferred his credits to a private academy (Bending Oaks) in Dallas. There, he took a couple of make-up courses and graduated on time. Armstrong had already bought his graduation cap and gown and prom tickets at Plano East, and although he didn't graduate there, he did attend the prom.

Other notables who were born in North Texas and/or attended area Texas schools but who moved out of state or did not finish high school for various reasons:

- Pop singer Jessica Simpson attended J. J. Pearce High School in Richardson in the mid-1990s. She was named Homecoming Queen both as a sophomore and as a junior. Simpson dropped out of school prior to the start of her senior year to pursue her musical career. She later earned her General Equivalency Diploma (GED) through correspondence courses from Texas Tech University.
- Robert Van Winkle, better known as rapper Vanilla Ice,

attended R. L. Turner High School in Carrollton in the 1980s but did not graduate. He is best known for the number one song "Ice Ice Baby."

- Country singer Roger Miller was born in Fort Worth but moved to Oklahoma as a child.
- Gene Autry, the first singing cowboy, was born and raised in Tioga. He attended Tioga schools until he and his family moved to Oklahoma during his senior year in high school.
- Country singer LeAnn Rimes dropped out of junior high school in Garland after signing a recording contract. She later took high school correspondence courses through Texas Tech University.
- Blues guitarist Stevie Ray Vaughan dropped out of Dallas Kimball High School after the fall semester of his senior year (1971).
- World War II hero Audie Murphy quit school following the fifth grade. He attended Celeste schools for four years and the Floyd School for one year.
- Actor Robby Benson was born in Dallas but grew up in New York City. He graduated as valedictorian from the prestigious Lincoln Square Academy.
- Rock musician Stephen Stills (Crosby, Stills, Nash, and Young) was born in Dallas but attended high school in the Republic of Panama and Costa Rica.
- Pro golfer Byron Nelson quit school during his sophomore year in Dallas.
- Pro golfer Ben Hogan was absent 65 days of the 90-day second semester at Fort Worth Central High School. He received no credits and left without graduating.
- Sylvester Stewart of Sly and The Family Stone musical fame is a Dallas native. He graduated from high school in Vallejo, California.
- President Dwight D. Eisenhower was born in Denison but moved with his family to Kansas while an infant. He graduated from Abilene (Kan.) High School in 1909.
- Hall of Fame baseball player Joe Morgan was born in Bonham (Fannin County).

At the age of five, Morgan and his family moved to Oakland, California. He graduated from Oakland Castlemont High School.

- Olympic decathlon champion Rafer Johnson was born in Hillsboro and lived in the Oak Cliff section of Dallas as a child. At age nine he moved with his family to California.
- Country musician Buck Owens was born in Sherman but as a child moved with his family to Arizona.
- Longtime U.S. Speaker of the House Sam Rayburn was born in Tennessee but moved to Fannin County in North Texas as a child. He attended Burnett Elementary School and completed his public school studies at the Flag Springs School, located a few miles southeast of Bonham.
- Pro golfer Lee Trevino quit school in Dallas following the seventh grade to go to work. He would have attended Dallas Hillcrest High School.
- Hall of Fame baseball player Rogers Hornsby attended Fort Worth North Side in the early 1900s before quitting to go to work.

Vocabulary

Pep rally — an organized activity in which students, cheerleaders, band, and others show their support for a school's athletic team prior to a game.

Cheerleaders

- Phyllis George, Denton
- Boz Scaggs, St. Mark's
- Susan Howard, Marshall
- Jerry Hall, Mesquite
- Michael Martin Murphey, Dallas Adamson
- Bill Moyers, Marshall
- Aaron Spelling, Dallas Forest Avenue
- Tracy Scoggins, Dickinson
- Kay Bailey, LaMarque
- Lee Ann Womack, Jacksonville

Bending Oaks Academy (Dallas)

LANCE ARMSTRONG
(1990)
Four-time
Tour de France winner

Carrollton R. L. Turner High

ROBERT VAN WINKLE

VANILLA ICE
Rap singer
"Ice Ice Baby"

High School Confidential

Brian Bosworth, who went on to fame as a football player at the University of Oklahoma and later the Seattle Seahawks, was suspended for three days from Irving MacArthur High School for his involvement in a food fight in the school cafeteria.

Dallas W. H. Adamson High

JIM WRIGHT
(1939)
U.S. congressman
Speaker of the House

Dallas W. H. Adamson High

RAY PRICE
(1946)
Country musician
"For the Good Times"

Dallas W. H. Adamson High

MICHAEL MARTIN
MURPHEY
(1963)
Country musician
"Wildfire"

Dallas W. H. Adamson High

RAY HUBBARD
(1965)

RAY WYLIE HUBBARD
Country musician
"Up Against the Wall,
Redneck Mother"

Dallas W. H. Adamson High

CHUCK STEVENSON
(1967)

B. W. STEVENSON
Musician
"My Maria"

Dallas N. R. Crozier Tech High

TRINI LOPEZ
Singer
"If I Had A Hammer"
"La Bamba"

Dallas N. R. Crozier Tech High

DOMINGO SAMUDIO
Leader of the rock group
Sam the Sham and the
Pharaohs
"Li'l Red Riding Hood"

Dallas Forest Avenue High (Now Madison High)

STANLEY MARCUS
(1921)
Businessman
Neiman-Marcus
Department Store

High School Confidential

*Miller Barber won 11 tournaments on the Professional
Golfers' Association (PGA) Tour and another 24 events on
the Senior PGA Tour. A longtime resident of Sherman,
Texas, Barber was born in Shreveport, Louisiana. He grew
up in Texarkana, Texas, where he graduated from Texas
High School in 1949. He then graduated from the University of Arkansas. A classmate of Barber's at Texas High was
future businessman Ross Perot. While still active on the pro
golf tour in the 1980s, Barber was elected to serve as a member of the Sherman ISD School Board.*

Dallas Forest Avenue High (Now Madison High)

AARON SPELLING
(1939)
Television producer
Charlie's Angels

Dallas Thomas Jefferson High

BRENDA VACARRO
(1958)
Actress

Dallas Thomas Jefferson High

MICHAEL NESMITH
(1961)
Member of the Monkees
pop group

Dallas Thomas Jefferson High

MARVIN LEE ADAY
(1966)

MEAT LOAF
Rock musician/actor

Dallas Justin F. Kimball High

STEVIE VAUGHAN

STEVIE RAY VAUGHAN
Rock/blues musician

North Dallas High

FREDERICK BEAN
AVERY
(1926)

TEX AVERY
Cartoonist

North Dallas High

H. B. SANDERS
(1942)
"Barefoot" Sanders
U.S. Federal Judge

Dallas L. V. Pinkston High

REGINA TAYLOR
(1977)
Actress
I'll Fly Away

Dallas Skyline High

MICHAEL JOHNSON
(1986)
Olympic sprinter

Dallas Skyline High

LARRY JOHNSON
(1987)
Pro basketball player

Dallas South Oak Cliff High

DENNIS RODMAN
(1976)
Pro basketball player

Dallas Sunset High

DONALD JANUARY
(1947)

DON JANUARY
Pro golfer
PGA champion

63

Dallas Booker T. Washington High

ERNIE BANKS
(1949)
Hall of Fame baseball
player

Dallas Booker T. Washington High for the Visual and Performing Arts

EDIE BRICKELL
(1984)
Rock musician
Edie Brickell & the New
Bohemians
"What I Am"

Dallas Booker T. Washington High for the Visual and Performing Arts

ROY HARGROVE, JR.
(1988)
Jazz trumpeter

Dallas Booker T. Washington High for the Visual and Performing Arts

ERICA WRIGHT
(1989)

ERYKAH BADU
R & B musician

Dallas W. T. White High

KAREN ELIZABETH
PARFITT
(1975)

KAREN HUGHES
Former counselor to
George W. Bush

Dallas Woodrow Wilson High

RALPH GULDAHL
(1930)
Pro golfer, U.S. Open
and Masters champion

Dallas Woodrow Wilson High

ROBERT DAVID
O'BRIEN
(1935)

DAVEY O'BRIEN
Heisman Trophy winner

Dallas Woodrow Wilson High

STEVE MILLER
(1961)
Rock musician
"The Joker"

Dallas Woodrow Wilson High

TIM BROWN
(1984)
Heisman Trophy winner

Denison St. Xavier's Academy

JACK HILLERMAN
(1949)

JOHN HILLERMAN
Actor
Magnum, P.I.

Denton High

PHYLLIS GEORGE
(1967)

PHYLLIS GEORGE
Miss America (1971)

Denton High

SHIRLEY COTHRAN
(1973)
Miss America (1975)

SHIRLEY COTHRAN
BARRET

Farmersville High

CHARLES WATSON
(1964)

TEX WATSON
Convicted of
Tate-LaBianca murders

Ft. Worth Arlington Heights High

LEE HARVEY OSWALD
Accused of assassinating
President John F.
Kennedy

Ft. Worth Arlington Heights High

HENRY JOHN
DEUTSCHENDORF
(1961)

JOHN DENVER
Pop musician
"Rocky Mountain High"

Ft. Worth Arlington Heights High

BETTY BUCKLEY
(1964)
Actress
Eight is Enough,
Tender Mercies,
Cats (on Broadway)

Ft. Worth Arlington Heights High

BILL PAXTON
(1973)
Actor
Titanic,
Twister,
Apollo 13

Ft. Worth Central High (now Robert Lee Paschal High)

BEN HOGAN
Professional golfer/
Grand Slam winner

Ft. Worth North Side High

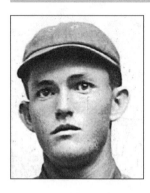

ROGERS HORNSBY
Hall of Fame baseball player

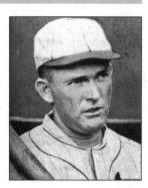

Ft. Worth North Side High

JOHNNY
RUTHERFORD
(1956)
Indy 500 racecar winner

Ft. Worth Robert Lee Paschal High

LIZ SMITH
(1940)
Newspaper columnist

Ft. Worth Robert Lee Paschal High

DAN JENKINS
(1948)
Author
Semi-Tough

Ft. Worth Robert Lee Paschal High

ALAN BEAN
(1956)

CAPTAIN ALAN BEAN
Astronaut

Ft. Worth Robert Lee Paschal High

JOE DON LOONEY
(1960)
Pro football player

Grand Prairie Dal-Worth High

CHARLEY TAYLOR
(1960)
Pro football Hall of Fame
receiver

Highland Park High

WILLIAM P. CLEMENTS JR.
(1934)
Texas governor

Highland Park High

BOBBY LAYNE
(1944)
Hall of Fame football
player

Highland Park High

DOAK WALKER
(1945)
Heisman Trophy winner

Highland Park High

VERA JAYNE PEERS
(1950)

JAYNE MANSFIELD
Actress

Highland Park High

JOHN HINCKLEY JR.
(1973)
Accused of wounding
President Ronald Reagan

Highland Park High

ANGIE HARMON
(1990)
Model/actress
Law & Order

The Hockaday School

PATRICIA RICHARDSON
(1969)
TV actress
Home Improvement

The Hockaday School

LISA LOEB
Singer/songwriter
"Stay (I Missed You)"

Irving MacArthur High

BRIAN BOSWORTH
(1983)
Football player/actor

Lewisville High

WALT GARRISON
(1962)
Pro football player
Dallas Cowboys

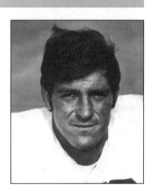

North Mesquite High

JERRY HALL
(1973)
Model/actress

75

Pilot Point Gee High

G. A. MOORE JR.
(1957)
Record-setting Texas
high school football coach

Plano High

GREG RAY
(1984)
Racecar driver

Richardson High

ANN O'BRIEN
(1959)

ANNE RICE
Author
The Vampire Chronicles

Richardson Lake Highlands High

PATSY MCCLENNY
(1968)

MORGAN FAIRCHILD
Actress

Richardson Lake Highlands High

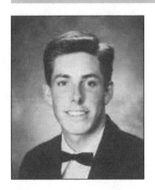

JUSTIN LEONARD
(1990)
Professional golfer,
British Open Champion

St. Mark's School of Texas

BILL SCAGGS
(1962)

BOZ SCAGGS
Musician
Silk Degrees

St. Mark's School of Texas

TOMMY JONES
(1965)

TOMMY LEE JONES
Actor
The Executioner's Song

Weatherford High

LARRY HAGMAN
(1949)
Actor
J. R. Ewing
Dallas

High School Confidential

The Mesquite High School band plays a memorable fight song when its team scores. It's the same fight song ("Texas Taps") as that of the University of Texas.

High School Confidential

Country musician Waylon Jennings was expelled from his music class at Littlefield High School for lack of musical ability. He dropped out of high school in the tenth grade.

High School Confidential

Capt. Alan Bean took a flag from his alma mater (Ft. Worth Paschal) with him to the moon on Apollo 12. The flag is now displayed at the school.

Not Pictured:

Denton High
ANN SHERIDAN
(1933)
Actress *King's Row*

Ft. Worth Arlington Heights High
T. CULLEN DAVIS
(1951)
Businessman

Ft. Worth Arlington Heights High
THOMAS THOMPSON
(1951)
Author *Celebrity*

Ft. Worth Central High
(Now Paschal High)

VIRGINIA KATHERINE MCMATH
GINGER ROGERS
Actress/dancer

Weatherford High
MARY MARTIN
(1931)
Dancer/actress *Peter Pan*

Weatherford High School
1949 Yearbook

Greetings, congratulations and good wishes to the Melon Vine of 1949 as it seeks to portray as well as preserve the life of Weatherford High School as it is enacted day by day. No amount of money would buy the benefit that has come to me personally through the fellowship and friendship of the students of Weatherford High School. I shall always cherish your memory.

J. E. GRANSTAFF
Principal

Cheerleaders Candids

A member of the LaMarque High School cheerleading squad in 1960-61 was Kay Bailey top, left. Kay Bailey became Kay Bailey Hutchison and was elected to the United States

Future Oscar-winning actress Sissy Spacek (right) was a cheerleader at Quitman High School.

In the early 1960s, before "Harper Valley PTA," Jeanne Stephenson (now known as Jeannie C. Riley) was Head Majorette at Anson High School.

Cheering on the Jacksonville High School Tigers in the early 1980s was Lee Ann Womack.

Future actress Tracy Scoggins (standing, left) was a Dickinson High School cheerleader.

Michael Martin Murphy, second from right, bottom row, was a cheerleader at Dallas Adamson. He later became a country musician.

Future Miss America Phyllis George (far left) was a member of the Denton High School cheerleading squad in the late 1960s.

Down Memory Lane: The Music

Most Popular Songs, Year-by-Year

1937—"Sweet Leilani," Bing Crosby

1938—"A-Tisket, A-Tasket," Ella Fitzgerald

1939—"Deep Purple," Larry Clinton with Chuck Webb

1940—"Frenesi," Artie Shaw

1941—"Amapola," Jimmy Dorsey

1942—"White Christmas," Bing Crosby

1943—"I've Heard that Song Before," Harry James

1944—"Swinging on a Star," Bing Crosby

1945—"Rum and Coca-Cola," Andrews Sisters

1946—"The Gypsy," Ink Spots

1947—"Near You," Francis Craig

1948—"Buttons and Bows," Dinah Shore

1949—"Riders in the Sky," Vaughn Monroe

1950—"The Tennessee Waltz," Patti Page

1951—"Cry," Johnnie Ray

1952—"You Belong to Me," Jo Stafford

1953—"Vaya Con Dios," Les Paul and Mary Ford

1954—"Sh-Boom," Crew-Cuts

1955—"Rock Around the Clock," Bill Haley and the Comets

1956—"Don't Be Cruel"/"Hound Dog," Elvis Presley

1957—"All Shook Up," Elvis Presley

1958—"At the Hop," Danny and the Juniors

1959—"Mack The Knife," Bobby Darin

1960—"Theme from A Summer Place," Percy Faith

1961—"Tossin & Turnin," Bobby Lewis

1962—"I Can't Stop Loving You," Ray Charles

1963—"Sugar Shack," Jimmy Gilmer and the Fireballs

1964—"I Wanna Hold Your Hand," The Beatles

1965—"Satisfaction," Rolling Stones

1966—"I'm a Believer," The Monkees

1967—"To Sir With Love," Lulu

1968—"Hey Jude," The Beatles

1969—"Aquarius"/"Let the Sun Shine In," Fifth Dimension

1970—"Bridge Over Troubled Water," Simon & Garfunkel

1971—"Joy to the World," Three Dog Night

1972—"The First Time Ever I Saw Your Face," Roberta Flack

1973—"Killing Me Softly With His Song," Roberta Flack

1974—"The Way We Were," Barbra Streisand

1975—"Love Will Keep Us Together," Captain and Tennille

1976—"Tonight's the Night," Rod Stewart

1977—"You Light Up My Life," Debby Boone

1978—"Night Fever," Bee Gees

1979—"My Sharona," The Knack

1980—"Lady," Kenny Rogers

1981—"Physical," Olivia Newton-John

1982—"I Love Rock and Roll," Joan Jett and the Blackhearts

1983—"Every Breath You Take," Police

1984—"Like a Virgin," Madonna

1985—"Say You, Say Me," Lionel Richie

1986—"That's What Friends Are For," Dionne and Friends

1987—"Faith," George Michael

1988—"Roll With It," Steve Winwood

1989—"Another Day in Paradise," Phil Collins

1990—"Nothing Compares 2 U," Sinead O'Connor

1991—"I Do It For You," Bryan Adams

1992—"End of the Road," Boyz II Men

1993—"Dreamlover," Mariah Carey

1994—"The Sign," Ace of Base

1995—"Gangsta's Paradise," Coolio, featuring L. V.

1996—"Macarena," Los Del Rio

1997—"Candle in the Wind," Elton John

1998—"Too Close," Next

1999—"Believe," Cher

2000—"Breathe," Faith Hill

2001—"Hanging by a Moment," Lighthouse

Junior

East Texas

Reform School

"*Seventy-five percent of high school seniors don't know who Whitman or Thoreau is. Twenty-five percent of college seniors in Texas can't name the country on Texas's southern border. That's scary.*"

— Billionaire businessman and education reform leader H. Ross Perot, 1988

Kilgore High 1953 Yearbook

K. H. S.
1933 - 1953

REFLECTO

STAFF

Carol Terry
Editor

Hyman Laufer
Sponsor

Rosemary Butts
Artist

Davie Lou Ettelman

Jan Park

Jimmy Hutchison

Lucretia Austin

Jimmy Athey

John Schuh

Virginia Looney

KILGORE HIGH SC

KILGORE, TEXAS

No individual has done more to shake up public education in Texas than billionaire businessman and two-time presidential candidate H. Ross Perot (Texarkana Texas High, '47).

Having already made his fortune in the computer business, Perot was appointed by Gov. Mark White (Houston Lamar, '58) to head the Governor's Select Committee on Public Education in 1983.

Perot and company traveled the state to visit with educators, business leaders, and citizens to determine the ills of the public education system. He quickly targeted extracurricular activities — particularly football — as taking too much time away from the academic focus.

Perot and company presented several controversial proposals to Gov. White. And after much lobbying on the part of Perot and company, House Bill 72, complete with sweeping education reforms, was passed by the Texas Legislature in 1984.

Among the key features of the bill were the "no-pass, no play" rule for students in extracurricular activities, smaller class sizes, revision of the state funding system to provide more aid to property-poor districts, teacher pay raises, a controversial "career ladder" pay system, a requirement that teachers pass a basic skills test in reading and writing to retain employment, and a teacher appraisal system.

In pushing the legislation through with an abrasive and dictatorial style, Perot drew the wrath of many administrators, teachers, and coaches. Teachers were insulted by having to take the basic skills test, while coaches were enraged by the "no-pass, no-play" rule. "Will Rogers never met Ross Perot" and "I Don't Brake for Ross Perot" bumper stickers were printed and distributed throughout the state. And coaches wore red dots on their wristwatches to remind themselves to vote against Gov. White.

Other critics pointed out that Perot did not participate in extracurricular activities while in high school and that all of his children attended private school.

Gov. White, thanks in great part to the controversial education reforms, was defeated in his re-election bid in 1986.

Time has proven that some of the reforms were beneficial; however, many were failures. In addition, some of the mandates were not funded by the state, and local districts endured additional financial burdens.

Join the Club

A list of common clubs and organizations found in Texas high schools:

DECA — Distributive Education Clubs of America

FCA — Fellowship of Christian Athletes

FFA — Future Farmers of America

FHA — Future Homemakers of America

FTA — Future Teachers of America

JCL — Junior Classical League

HOSA — Health Occupations Students of America

NHS — National Honor Society

PASF — Pan-American Student Forum

ROTC — Reserve Officer Training Corps

VICA — Vocational Industrial Clubs of America

Art Club

Beta Club

Chess Club

Forensic League

French Club

Glee Club

HI-Y

Key Club

Pep Club

Quill & Scroll

Science Club

Slide Rule Club

Thespians

East Texas high schools may not compete with their big-city counterparts in terms of quantity of graduates, but quality is another matter.

Emerging from schools in the region have been back-to-back future Heisman Trophy winners, a First Lady, a billionaire businessman, a world renowned classical pianist, a big city mayor, a top flight rock 'n' roll musician, and a pair of outstanding pro football quarterbacks.

In 1973, a running back-linebacker named Earl Campbell led the Tyler John Tyler Lions to the state football championship. Campbell went on to star at the University of Texas, winning the Heisman Trophy in 1977. The following year, the Heisman was captured by University of Oklahoma running back Billy Sims, a 1975 graduate of tiny Hooks High School.

Back in 1928, Claudia Taylor graduated third in her class (at age 15) at Marshall High School. In later years, she would be known as Lady Bird Johnson, wife of President Lyndon B. Johnson.

Earning a diploma in 1947 at Texarkana Texas High School was former newspaper delivery boy Henry Ross Perot. In high school, Perot was the yearbook business manager, but he showed few signs of future brilliance. He was a "B" student and was described by classmates as "ordinary." Many years later, he made a fortune in the computer business in Dallas.

The 1951 graduating class at Kilgore High School included young Van Cliburn. While attending KHS, Cliburn participated in band and drama. He was also voted "Most Ambitious" by his classmates. Cliburn's classical piano talents would win him the highest honors in international competition.

Current San Francisco mayor Willie Brown is a Mineola McFarland High School ('52) grad.

One of the founding members of the California rock group The Eagles was Don Henley, a 1965 graduate of Linden-Kildare High School. Henley was a member of the high school band and the Ag Club while in high school.

Two of the more well-known pro quarterbacks to come out of East Texas were Y. A. Tittle of Marshall High School ('44) and Don Meredith of Mt. Vernon High School ('56). Tittle played collegiately at Louisiana State University before starring for the New York Giants in the National Football League. Meredith took his free spirit to Southern Methodist University and later led the Dallas Cowboys to respectability. After retiring early from pro football, Meredith found fame as a color analyst on ABC-TV's *Monday Night Football*. He also acted in films and television.

Country music crooner Jim Reeves was a standout baseball player at Carthage High School ('41) and was awarded a baseball scholarship to the University of Texas. His life was cut short by a plane crash in 1964.

In more recent years, Jacksonville High School has produced country singers Neal McCoy ('76) and Lee Ann Womack ('84).

- Pop singer Johnny Nash was born in Gilmer. As a child, he moved with this family to San Francisco, where he graduated from George Washington High School.
- Country singer Lefty Frizzell was born in Corsicana. He never advanced past sixth grade, dropping out of the Greenville school system after only two days of classes.

Sulphur Springs Yearbook

Football

Hooray for Hollywood
(High)

Arguably the most famous high school outside the state of Texas (excluding Columbine, Colorado) is Hollywood (Ca.) High School.

The school was built in an opportune time (1905) and in an opportune place (at the corner of Sunset Boulevard and Highland Avenue). In 1911, the movie industry came to town.

For some 90 years now, Hollywood High School has provided the entertainment industry with talent.

Talent scouts often sit in on school plays, debates and contests, hoping to make a "discovery."

In 1936, the school was placed on the map when one of its students — sophomore Judy Turner — skipped a typing class to run across the street and get a soda. After the "discovery" of Lana Turner, Hollywood High was dubbed "The Star Hatchery." In 1936 alone, classmates at HH included Turner, Mickey Rooney, Judy Garland, and Nanette Fabray.

Among other notables attending Hollywood High over the years were Fay Wray, Sally Kellerman, James Garner, Joel McCrea, Jason Robards, Rick Nelson, John Ritter, Stefanie Powers, Linda Evans, Tuesday Weld, Meredith Baxter Birney, Charlene Tilton, and Carol Burnett.

Burnett, who graduated in 1951, had attended elementary school in San Antonio, Texas, before moving with her family to California.

Paris High Yearbook

"The Guiding Light"

Left to right:
First row: Bebes Stallings, Larry Bell, Tommy Haynes.
Second row: Mary Cozort, Jackie Burch.
Third row: Sammy Player, Palmer Poteet.
Fourth row: Cleta Fae Kirtley, Philip Cecil.
Fifth row: Freddie Graham, J. T. Davis.
Sixth row: Don Coker, Doug Robinson, Noel Kelley.
Seventh row: Ruth Ann Jack, Herschel McCormick, John Fuston.

STUDENT COUNCIL

Not only does this organization supply enjoyment for the students, but it is also character building. It encouraged proper school conduct; its members gave the inspiring assembly prayers; it directed the first Career Day for Paris High School; it urged us daily to become better citizens of the future by sponsoring many worthwhile activities in which the student body participated and thus became more closely united. To see that the Student Council business is carried out more efficiently, the Council elected Charles Thompson as Chaplain, Linda Crawford as Corresponding Secretary; Ben Faber as Parliamentarian, and Butch Ellis as Reporter.

Since the Student Council was organized in P.H.S. it has inaugurated ideas and projects which are the traditions of our school today—traditions founded upon the ideals of leadership, scholarship, service, sportsmanship, and co-operation. And as the time goes on our Student Council is sure to become of even greater value to our school and community.

OWL 145

93

The Homefield Advantage

For years, the Wichita Falls High School Coyotes played in what was known as "Coyote Canyon." Most opponents conceded that Coyote Stadium, located on the old Seymour Highway, gave the home team a two-touchdown advantage. (The Coyotes just happened to be one of the most successful teams in the 1940s, '50s, and '60s.) The playing field was built below street level (as if it were at the bottom of a canyon), and the rowdy and unruly home team fans stood behind the visitors' bench, yelling and hollering at the players. The only thing that separated the bench from the elevated stands was a fence. Between the fence and the first row, a group of fans perched on stepladders as they hurled their insults. To make matters worse, the visitors' dressing room was a hole in the wall that sat underneath the stands directly beneath the Wichita Falls student section and band.

Things change, however, and by 1970, the Wichita Falls school district had built the $250,000 Memorial Stadium, which featured the first high school field in the world with artificial turf. Today, the "Canyon" is utilized by the school district as a bus parking lot.

Vocabulary

Assembly — an official gathering of students for a specific purpose, i.e., to listen to a guest speaker or musical program.

The Arts

- Patrick Swayze, Houston Waltrip (folk singing, drama)

- Ellen Smith (Jaclyn Smith), Houston Lamar (drama)

- Vera Jayne Peers (Jayne Mansfield), Highland Park (orchestra)

- Walter Cronkite, Houston San Jacinto (band)

- Linda Ellerbee, Houston Lamar (drama)

- Lyndon B. Johnson, Johnson City (debate)

- Buddy Holly, Lubbock (choir)

- Janis Joplin, Port Arthur Jefferson (art)

- Michael Nesmith, Dallas Thomas Jefferson (choir)

- Stanley Marcus, Dallas (orchestra)

- Henry John Deutschendorf (John Denver), Fort Worth Arlington Heights (choir)

- Phyllis George, Denton (choir, drama)

- J. P. Richardson Jr., Beaumont (choir)

- B. J. Thomas, Lamar Consolidated (choir)

- Marvin Lee Aday (Meat Loaf), Dallas Thomas Jefferson (drama)

- Johnny Lee, Santa Fe (band)

- Bill Moyers, Marshall (band)

- Dorothy Ann Willis a.k.a. Ann Richards, Waco High (debate)

- Roy Orbison, Wink (choir, band)

- Don Henley, Linden-Kildare (band)

- Barbara Jordan, Houston Wheatley (choir, debate)

- Larry Gatlin, Odessa High (all-state choir)

- Woodard "Tex" Ritter, Beaumont South Park (debate, drama)

- Tommy Tune, Houston Lamar (drama)

- Charles "Tex" Watson, Farmersville (drama)
- Horton Foote, Wharton (drama)
- John Connally, Floresville (debate)
- Tom Landry, Mission (band, choir)
- Jeri Lynn Mooney, a.k.a. Susan Howard, Marshall (drama)
- Van Cliburn, Kilgore (band, drama)
- Erica Wright, a.k.a. Erykah Badu, Booker T. Washington (dance)
- George W. Bush, Houston Kinkaid (debate)

- Bob Bullock, Hillsboro (band, orchestra)
- Ronnie Dunn, Port Isabel (band)
- Jeannie Stephenson, Anson High (band, head majorette, twirler)
- Henry Cisneros, San Antonio Central Catholic High (band)
- Trini Lopez, Dallas Crozier Tech (band)
- Domingo Samudio, Dallas Crozier Tech (art)
- Stevie Ray Vaughan, Dallas Kimball (art)

Arp High

GUY V. LEWIS
(1940)
College basketball coach
University of Houston

Carthage High

JIM REEVES
(1941)
Country musician
"He'll Have to Go"

Hooks High

BILLY SIMS
(1975)
Heisman Trophy winner

97

Jacksonville High

NEAL MCGAUGHEY
(1976)

NEAL MCCOY
Country musician
"No Doubt About It,"
"Wink"

Jacksonville High

LEE ANN WOMACK
(1984)
Country musician
"I Hope You Dance"

Kilgore High

VAN CLIBURN
(1951)
Internationally renowned
classical pianist; winner of
Tchaikovsky International
Piano Competition in
1958

Linden-Kildare High

DON HENLEY
(1965)
Rock musician, founding
member of The Eagles

Longview High

MATTHEW
MCCONAUGHEY
(1987)
Movie actor

High School Confidential

While attending Linden-Kildare High School in the mid-1960s, Don Henley was a member of the Future Farmers of America (FFA). His senior project in FFA was an acre and a half of cucumbers.

Marshall High

CLAUDIA TAYLOR
(1928)

LADY BIRD JOHNSON
First Lady

Marshall High

Y. A. TITTLE
(1944)
Pro quarterback

Marshall High

BILLY DON MOYERS
(1952)

BILL MOYERS
Press secretary to
President Lyndon B.
Johnson/journalist

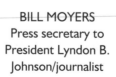

Marshall High

JERI LYNN MOONEY
(1964)

SUSAN HOWARD
TV actress, *Dallas*

Mineola McFarland School

WILLIE BROWN
(1952)
Mayor of San Francisco

Mt. Vernon High

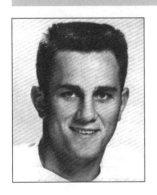

DON MEREDITH
(1956)
Dallas Cowboys
quarterback/actor

High School Confidential

Former Dallas Cowboys quarterback Don Meredith was an outstanding all-around athlete in the mid-1950s at Mt. Vernon High School. Meredith scored 52 points to set a single game scoring record in the Dr Pepper Basketball Tournament in Dallas.

Paris High

RAYMOND BERRY, JR.
(1950)
Pro football player/coach

Paris High

BEBES STALLINGS
(1953)

GENE STALLINGS
College/pro football
coach

Quitman High

SISSY SPACEK
(1968)
Movie actress

Sulphur Springs High

FORREST GREGG
(1952)
Hall of Fame pro football
player/coach

Terrell High

Terrell High
JAMIE FOXX
(1986)
Actor

Texas (Texarkana) High

H. ROSS PEROT
(1947)
Businessman/presidential
candidate

Texas (Texarkana) High

MILLER BARBER
(1949)
Professional golfer

Tyler Robert E. Lee High

SANDY DUNCAN
(1964)
Actress

Tyler John Tyler High

RALPH YARBOROUGH
U.S. senator

Tyler John Tyler High

EARL CAMPBELL
(1974)
Heisman Trophy winner

Not Pictured:

Tyler John Tyler High
JO-CARROLL DENNISON
Miss America 1942

Arts Candids

Van Cliburn plays the piano in this photo from the Kilgore High School yearbook. Cliburn won the Tchaikovsky International Piano Competition in 1958.

The president of the Lamar Consolidated High School choir in 1959 was B. J. Thomas. Thomas went on to record a number of pop hits in the 1970s.

Powers Boothe stars in the 1965 Snyder High School production of The Importance of Being Earnest. Boothe made his mark in the movies, starring as Jim Jones in Guyana: An American Tragedy.

Tracy Byrd of Vidor High, future country singer.

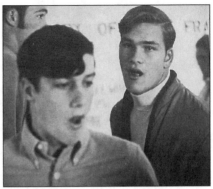

Future actor Patrick Swayze, right, as a student at Waltrip High in Houston.

Patsy McClenny, later known as actress Morgan Fairchild, studies at Richardson Lake Highlands High.

Future U.S. senator Kay Bailey in a dramatic scene at LaMarque High.

107

Down Memory Lane: Television

Most Popular Shows by Year

1950-51 — Texaco Star Theater

1951-52 — Arthur Godfrey's Talent Scouts

1952-53 — I Love Lucy

1953-54 — I Love Lucy

1954-55 — I Love Lucy

1955-56 — The $64,000 Question

1956-57 — I Love Lucy

1957-58 — Gunsmoke

1958-59 — Gunsmoke

1959-60 — Gunsmoke

1960-61 — Gunsmoke

1961-62 — Wagon Train

1962-63 — The Beverly Hillbillies

1963-64 — The Beverly Hillbillies

1964-65 — Bonanza

1965-66 — Bonanza

1966-67 — Bonanza

1967-68 — The Andy Griffith Show

1968-69 — Rowan & Martin's Laugh-In

1969-70 — Rowan & Martin's Laugh-In

1970-71 — Marcus Welby, M.D.

1971-72 — All in the Family

1972-73 — All in the Family

1973-74 — All in the Family

1974-75 — All in the Family

1975-76 — All in the Family

1976-77 — Happy Days

1977-78 — Laverne & Shirley

1978-79 — Laverne & Shirley

1979-80 — 60 Minutes

1980-81 — Dallas

1981-82 — Dallas

1982-83 — 60 Minutes

1983-84 — Dallas

1984-85 — Dynasty

1985-86 — The Cosby Show

1986-87 — The Cosby Show

1987-88 — The Cosby Show

1988-89 — The Cosby Show

1989-90 — The Cosby Show

1990-91 — Cheers

1991-92 — 60 Minutes

1992-93 — 60 Minutes

1993-94 — 60 Minutes

1994-95 — Seinfeld

1995-96 — ER

1996-97 — ER

1997-98 — Seinfeld

1998-99 — ER

1999-2000 — Who Wants to be a Millionaire?

2000-01 — Survivor

Senior

Central Texas

All the Way with LBJ

"My mother sat up all night at a house on North Astor trying to get me to memorize enough plane geometry to get me admitted to college. I made seventy, and seventy was passing, and I never had another damned bit of use for plane geometry before and I never have since."

— Lyndon B. Johnson

Hillsboro High 1948 Yearbook

El 'Aguila
1948

Published by Students
of
HILLSBORO HIGH SCHOOL
Hillsboro, Texas

Editor-in-Chief
BETTY COOPER

Associate Editors
JEANETTE DAVIS
BILL VAUGHN

Literary Editors
BETTY RAINWATER
PATSY LITTLE
JOYCE KINARD

Art Editors
MARTHA FARQUHAR
BILLY BOB CHAMBERS
JUNE WALKER

Photographers
C. J. YOUNGBLOOD
O. J. GRIZZLE
BILL WOODSIDE

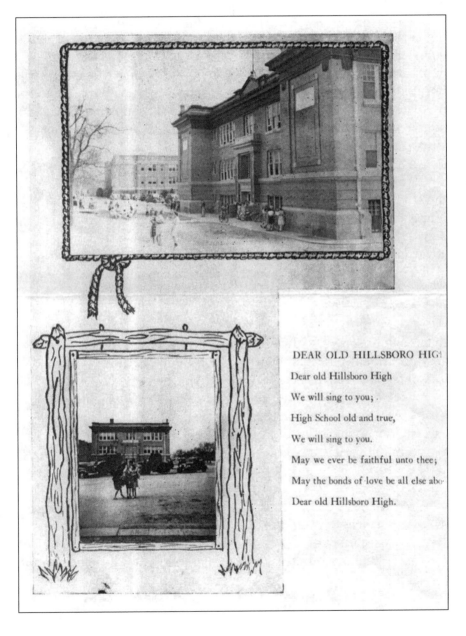

DEAR OLD HILLSBORO HIG¹

Dear old Hillsboro High

We will sing to you; .

High School old and true,

We will sing to you.

May we ever be faithful unto thee;

May the bonds of love be all else abo

Dear old Hillsboro High.

Lyndon Baines Johnson is arguably the most famous graduate of a Central Texas high school. In 1924, when Johnson was one of just six graduates of Johnson City High (located west of Austin), no one predicted that he would one day be the 36th President of the United States. But Johnson's classmates (four girls and one boy) weren't far off — as part of the traditional high school prophecy, the classmates predicted that he would one day be governor of Texas.

The Class of '24's motto was, "give the world the best you have and the best will come back to you."

Johnson's ambition and improbable rise to fame began at an early age. He was the youngest graduate (age fifteen) in school history. While in high school, Johnson participated in baseball and debate. He was also president of the junior class.

At that time, Johnson City High had only eleven grades, so it was not fully accredited. Johnson attended a six-week sub-college in order to "prove" his high school credits.

*****

Lyndon Johnson wasn't the only prominent public servant to hail from Central Texas.

Bob Bullock, who served as Texas secretary of state in the early 1970s and as a powerful lieutenant governor in the 1990s, was a Hillsboro High School graduate ('47).

Waco High School was home to future attorney/Watergate special prosecutor Leon Jaworski ('20) and Dorothy Ann Willis ('51).

Willis, better known as Ann Richards, was the first woman to hold the office of governor of Texas in her own right. She served in the office from 1991-95.

At Waco High, Willis participated in debate and was a Girls Nation delegate.

And then there's the pride of Abbott High School, Willie Nelson ('51). The country music superstar, who was a member of his high school football team, has returned home from time to time to perform benefit concerts. On November 4, 1973, Willie played a picnic during the Abbott homecoming to raise money for the school PTA.

And Austin high schools have provided their share of standouts over the years.

Stephen F. Austin High alums include reporter and White House press secretary Liz Carpenter ('38), baseball player-manager Don Baylor ('67), and pro golfer Ben Crenshaw ('70). Another top pro golfer — Tom Kite — graduated from Austin McCallum High School in 1968.

While Crenshaw and Kite concentrated on their golf

games in high school, Baylor was a standout in baseball, football, and basketball. He was also a member of the Junior Historians Club. And Carpenter edited the school paper at Austin High.

- Kenneth McDuff dropped out of school during his freshman year at Rosebud High in the early 1960s; later he would be arrested as one of Texas's most notorious serial killers.
- Comedian Steve Martin was born in Waco but graduated from high school in Garden Grove, Calif.

November 22, 1963

For today's students, the date September 11, 2001, will always be remembered as the day our nation was attacked by terrorists. Thousands of innocent people were killed, as airplanes crashed into the World Trade Center and the Pentagon.

For students in the 1960s, the date November 22, 1963, will always be remembered as the day President John F. Kennedy was assassinated. The president was fatally wounded by gunfire as he rode in a motorcade on the streets of downtown Dallas. Across the nation, students learned the tragic news through early afternoon news reports.

As one would expect, the news hit hard in Texas, where, prior to the tragedy, the president had been warmly greeted by crowds during his visit to the state.

On the day before the assassination, President Kennedy rode in a motorcade in San Antonio. Several students from San Antonio Central Catholic High School walked the few blocks from their campus to see the president. Among these students was a senior by the name of Henry Cisneros, who would later make a name for himself as the mayor of San Antonio and as the Secretary of Housing and Urban Development (HUD).

Meanwhile, back in Dallas, students were allowed (with a note from parents) to leave school to see the president. Among those choosing to do so was Dallas Thomas Jefferson student Marvin Lee Aday (today he's known as Meat Loaf). Aday and two friends drove to Love Field to see the president arrive. After grabbing lunch, the boys made a detour to a local bowling alley, where they heard the news of the president's shooting on a transistor radio. Like many others, they headed to Parkland Hospital to join a grieving crowd of spectators as President Kennedy and Texas Governor John Connally, who was wounded, were brought in.

Along with Henry Cisneros, these future Texas high school hotshots were seniors on November 22, 1963: Jeannie C. Riley of Anson High; Charles "Tex" Watson, Farmersville; Betty Buckley, Fort Worth Arlington Heights; Susan Howard, Marshall; Sandy Duncan, Tyler Robert E. Lee; Jaclyn Smith, Houston Lamar; Thomas Hicks, Port Arthur Jefferson; and Kenneth Starr, San Antonio Sam Houston.

Vocabulary

Homeroom — a designated room and period that students report to on a regular basis for non-instructional activities.

UIL Governs Extracurricular Activities

Based in Austin, the University Interscholastic League (UIL) is the largest interschool organization of its kind in the world. There are 1,280 UIL-member schools. The UIL sponsors 22 academic competitions, 10 music contests, and 22 athletic programs for boys and girls.

One out of every two graduating seniors in Texas will participate in one or more types of UIL-sponsored events while a student.

The UIL strives to provide healthy, character-building, educational activities, carried out under regulations voted on by school administrators. All rules and regulations that govern athletics and all other UIL activities are adopted by member schools and enforced by the UIL. The UIL was born in 1912 with the merger of the Texas Interscholastic Athletic Association and the Debating and Declamation League.

The purpose of the organization is stated in the preamble of an early issue of its constitution:

"...to foster among the schools of Texas inter-school competitions as an aid in the preparation for citizenship; to assist in organizing, standardizing and controlling athletics in the schools of the State; and to promote county, district and State interscholastic contests in debate, declamation, spelling, essay writing, arithmetic, writing, reading, extemporaneous speech, athletics and music memory."

Leaders

- Nolan Ryan, Alvin (Sophomore vice president)
- Bill Moyers, Marshall (Student Council)
- H. B. "Barefoot" Sanders, North Dallas (Student Council vice president)
- Boz Scaggs, St. Mark's (Junior Class vice president)
- Barbara Jordan, Houston Wheatley (National Honor Society president)
- Woodard "Tex" Ritter, Beaumont South Park (Senior Class president)
- William P. Clements Jr., Highland Park (Sophomore, Junior, Senior Class president)
- Lyndon B. Johnson, Johnson City (Junior Class president)
- Jack Mildren, Abilene Cooper (Freshman Class president)
- Ronnie Dunn, Port Isabel (Class vice president)
- Kay Bailey, LaMarque (Student Council)
- Jeannie Stephenson, Anson High (Student Council)
- Charles Stenholm, Stamford (Texas Future Farmers of America state president)
- John Mahaffey, Kerrville Tivy (Student Council)
- Sandra Day O'Connor, El Paso Austin (National Honor Society)
- Davey O'Brien, Dallas Woodrow Wilson (National Honor Society, Student Council)
- Gene Stallings, Paris (Student Council treasurer, FFA president, Junior Rotarian)

Abbott High

WILLIE NELSON
(1951)
Country musician

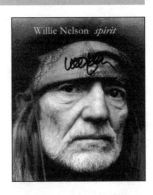

Austin Anderson High

THOMAS HENDERSON

**THOMAS
"HOLLYWOOD"
HENDERSON**
Professional football
player

Austin Stephen F. Austin High

LIZ CARPENTER
(1938)
Presidential press
secretary/journalist

117

Austin Stephen F. Austin High

DON BAYLOR
(1967)
Major League baseball
player/manager

Austin Stephen F. Austin High

BEN CRENSHAW
(1970)
Professional golfer/
Masters champion

Austin McCallum High

TOM KITE
(1968)
Professional golfer/
U.S. Open champion

Belton High

FORREST SHERROD
(1937)

BLACKIE SHERROD
Dallas sportswriter

Cameron Yoe High

ROBERT DRAYTON
MCLANE, JR.
(1954)

DRAYTON MCLANE
Businessman/owner of
Houston Astros

Hillsboro High

BOBBY BULLOCK
(1947)

BOB BULLOCK
Lieutenant governor
of Texas

Johnson City High

LYNDON B. JOHNSON
(1924)
36th President of United
States

Lampasas High

JOHNNY JONES
(1976)

JOHNNY "LAM" JONES
Olympic sprinter/football
player

Mexia High

VICKIE HOGAN

ANNA NICOLE SMITH
Model

Temple Dunbar High

JOE GREENE
(1965)
Hall of Fame pro football
player

Waco High

LEON JAWORSKI
(1920)
Attorney/Watergate
special prosecutor

High School Confidential

Vickie Hogan (a.k.a. Anna Nicole Smith), the model who married elderly billionaire J. Howard Marshall II, dropped out of Mexia High School in the 1980s after being expelled for fighting.

Waco High

DOROTHY ANN
WILLIS
(1951)

ANN RICHARDS
Governor of Texas

Not Pictured:

Austin L. C. Anderson High
DICK LANE
(1951)
DICK "NIGHT TRAIN" LANE
Hall of Fame football player

Groesbeck High
JOE DON BAKER
(1955)
Actor
Walking Tall

Leaders Candids

Quarterback Jack Mildren speaks at a pep rally at Abilene Cooper High School in 1967.

Included in this group photo from the 1920 Waco High School yearbook is Leon Jaworski. In the 1970s, Jaworski gained notoriety as the Watergate Special Prosecutor.

Neal McGaughey, later known as Neal McCoy, is shown at Jacksonville High School in 1976. In the 1990s McCoy recorded such country hits as "No Doubt About It" and "Wink."

123

Betty Buckley was involved in a number of activities at Fort Worth Arlington Heights High School. After graduating in 1964, she pursued a career in acting. Buckley was a regular on the *Eight is Enough* TV show, has appeared in numerous movies, and also performed in the Broadway play *Cats*.

Down Memory Lane: Texas Governors Year-by-Year

1846-1847 — J. Pinckney Henderson (Albert C. Horton served as Acting Governor while Henderson was serving in the Mexican War)

1847-1849 — George T. Wood

1849-1853 — Peter Hansbrough Bell

1853 — J. W. Henderson

1853-1857 — Elisha M. Pease

1857-1859 — Hardin R. Runnels

1859-1861 — Sam Houston

1861 — Edward Clark

1861-1863 — Francis R. Lubbock

1863-1865 — Pendleton Murrah

1865-1866 — Andrew J. Hamilton

1866-1867 — James W. Throckmorton

1867-1869 — Elisha M. Pease

1870-1874 — Edmund J. Davis

1874-1876 — Richard Coke

1876-1879 — Richard B. Hubbard

1879-1883 — Oran M. Roberts

1883-1887 — John Ireland

1887-1891 — Lawrence Sullivan Ross

1891-1895 — James Stephen Hogg

1895-1899 — Charles A. Culberson

1899-1903 — Joseph D. Sayers

1903-1907 — S. W. T. Lanham

1907-1911 — Thomas Mitchell Campbell

1911-1915 — Oscar Branch Colquitt

1915-1917 — James E. Ferguson

1917-1921 — William Pettus Hobby

1921-1925 — Pat Morris Neff

1925-1927 — Miriam A. Ferguson

1927-1931 — Dan Moody

1931-1933 — Ross S. Sterling

1933-1935 — Miriam A. Ferguson

1935-1939 — James B. Allred

1939-1941 — W. Lee O'Daniel

1941-1947 — Coke R. Stevenson

1947-1949 — Beauford H. Jester

1949-1957 — Allan Shivers

1957-1963 — Price Daniel

1963-1969 — John Connally

1969-1973 — Preston Smith

1973-1979 — Dolph Briscoe

1979-1983 — William P. Clements

1983-1987 — Mark White

1987-1991 — William P. Clements

1991-1995 — Ann W. Richards

1995-2001 — George W. Bush

2001 — Rick Perry

Graduate

South Texas

Beatniks, Jocks, and That's the Way It Is

"They laughed me out of class, out of town, and out of the state."

— Rock/blues singer Janis Joplin (Port Arthur
Jefferson, '60)

Port Arthur Jefferson High School Yearbook

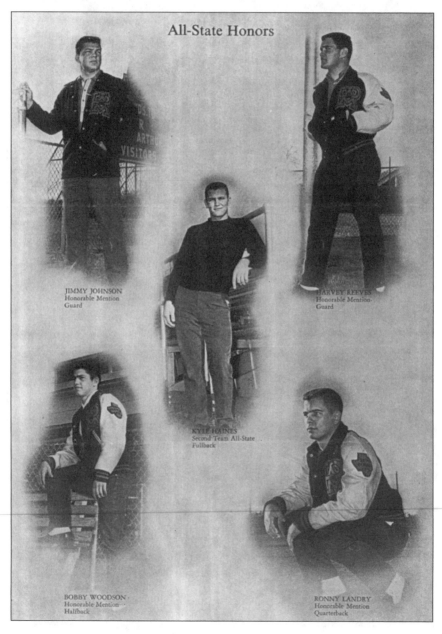

All-State Honors

JIMMY JOHNSON
Honorable Mention
Guard

HARVEY REEVES
Honorable Mention
Guard

KYLE HAINES
Second Team All-State
Fullback

BOBBY WOODSON
Honorable Mention
Halfback

RONNY LANDRY
Honorable Mention
Quarterback

Two of the students in the history class at Port Arthur Jefferson High School couldn't have been more opposite.

The year was 1960, and sitting at a desk in the classroom was a young athlete named Jimmy Johnson, who would one day be famous as coach of the world champion Dallas Cowboys. Sitting directly behind Johnson was a girl named Janis Joplin, who would become a famous San Francisco rock/blues singer and who would die of a drug overdose in 1969.

"Janis Lyn Joplin ran with what we called, in the late 1950s, the beatnik crowd," Johnson wrote in his 1993 book, *Turning the Thing Around*. "She wore black leotards, dark glasses, the whole bit. Her crowd was, to say the least, anti-jock...Janis looked and acted so weird that when we were around her, mostly in the hallways at school, we would give her a hard time...She graduated that spring of 1960, and we would never see each other again."

But don't get the impression that South Texas high schools have turned out only beatniks and jocks. There's the little matter of the evening news to consider.

No less than four area grads (Walter Cronkite, Dan Rather, Linda Ellerbee, and Jim Lehrer) at one time or another anchored national television news broadcasts.

News icon Cronkite ended each *CBS Evening News* presentation with the signature comment, "and that's the way it is." He graduated from Houston San Jacinto High School ('33), where, among other activities, he played in the band. (Another San Jacinto-ex is noted heart surgeon Dr. Denton Cooley ('37), who was also an outstanding basketball player.)

Cronkite's successor at CBS was none other than Dan Rather, a product of John Reagan High School ('50) in Houston. Rather played end on the Bulldogs football team, and one of his fondest memories is catching a game-winning pass against rival Milby High in 1949.

Other notables walking the halls at Reagan included future firefighter Red Adair and criminal defense attorney Richard

"Racehorse" Haynes. Adair, the famed oilfield firefighter, was a standout football player and swimmer. He dropped out of high school in the early 1930s to work at a drugstore to help support his family.

Linda Smith Ellerbee (Houston Mirabeau B. Lamar High School, '62) has hosted several national TV news broadcasts and shows over the years.

Other prominent Lamar grads are Broadway dancer Tommy Tune ('57), Gov. Mark White ('58), and actress Jaclyn Smith ('64).

And Jim Lehrer, who achieved notoriety on the Public Broadcasting System (PBS) news, is a graduate of Thomas Jefferson High School in San Antonio. Lehrer attended Beaumont French High School before transferring to Jefferson.

Two of the more famous names in Texas football history — Kyle Rote ('47) and Tommy Nobis ('62) — are also TJ graduates.

Other noteworthy sports figures who were educated in South Texas schools include baseball pitchers Nolan Ryan (Alvin High School, '65) and

Roger Clemens (Houston Spring Woods, '79); Heisman Trophy winner Andre Ware (Dickinson High School, '86); legendary NFL coaches Tom Landry (Mission High School, '42) and Oail "Bum" Phillips (Beaumont French, '42); and pro basketball star Shaquille O'Neal (San Antonio Cole, '90).

Hollywood has also benefited from the talents of a number of former South Texas students.

Actress Farrah Fawcett is a 1965 graduate of W. B. Ray High School in Corpus Christi. Actors and brothers Randy ('68) and Dennis ('72) Quaid were both students at Houston Bellaire.

S. P. Waltrip High School in Houston produced film stars Shelley Duvall ('67) and Patrick Swayze ('71). Meanwhile, over at Yates High School in Houston, sisters/actresses Phylicia Allen Rashad ('66) and Debbie Allen ('68) were members of the student body.

Several future musicians also studied at area schools. Among that group were country singer Woodard "Tex" Ritter, Beaumont South Park ('22); ZZ Top member Billy Gibbons,

Houston Robert E. Lee High ('67); country singer Lyle Lovett, Klein High ('75); country singer George Strait, Pearsall High School ('70); country singer Ronnie Dunn of Brooks & Dunn fame, Port Isabel High School ('71); pop-gospel singer B. J. Thomas, Lamar Consolidated High School in Rosenberg ('59); pop musician Christopher Cross, San Antonio Alamo Heights ('69); and rock-country wizard Doug Sahm, San Antonio Sam Houston ('60).

Houston Waltrip High School

Two NASCAR drivers, brothers Terry and Bobby Labonte, have Texas roots. Terry graduated from Corpus Christi Carroll High (1975), while younger brother Bobby followed the family to North Carolina, where he completed high school.

Several other prominent people attended area schools but either moved away before graduating or quit school for various reasons. That list includes:

- President George W. Bush attended the Kinkaid School (private academy) in Houston for two years (eighth and ninth grade) before transferring to the prestigious Phillips Academy in Andover, Maryland. At Phillips, he played baseball and basketball, was a member of the Spanish Club, and was head cheerleader. He graduated from Phillips in June 1964.

- Country singer Clint Black dropped out of Katy High School after his junior year (1980) to pursue a career in music.

- Country singer Johnny Lee found fame with his single "Lookin' for Love," which was featured in the 1980 movie *Urban Cowboy*. Lee

131

attended Santa Fe High School but dropped out during his sophomore year (1963) to join the Marines.

- Tejano singing star Selena was born in Corpus Christi. She left Corpus Christi West Oso Junior High in the eighth grade to pursue her singing career. Selena later received her high school diploma through correspondence courses from Chicago.

- Actor-musician Kris Kristofferson was born in Brownsville. His father was in the U.S. Air Force, and the family moved frequently. He graduated from San Mateo High School in California.

- Actress Carol Burnett was born in San Antonio, where she attended elementary school. She moved with her family to California and graduated from Hollywood High School.

- Although he was born in Marshall, heavyweight boxing champion George Foreman grew up in inner-city Houston. He dropped out of junior high school to join the Job Corps, where he discovered boxing.

- Country music singer Barbara Mandrell was born in Houston but moved to California as a child. She graduated from Oceanside (Ca.) High School.

- One of the all-time great female athletes — Babe Didrikson Zaharias — dropped out of Beaumont High School in 1930 to play semi-pro basketball.

- Country singer George Jones was born in Saratoga. He quit school in the seventh grade.

- Racecar driver A. J. Foyt dropped out of Houston Reagan at the beginning of his senior year.

- Actor Gary Busey was born in Goose Creek, Texas, but grew up in Oklahoma.

- Actress Meredith MacRae was born in Houston but graduated from Buckley High in Van Nuys, Ca.

- Country singer Mark Chesnutt quit school at Beaumont South Park when he was fifteen years old.

- Billionaire Howard Hughes attended South End Junior High in Houston before being sent east to boarding school and later to a private school in California.

- Oliver North was born in San Antonio but moved with his family to the East Coast. He is a graduate of Ockawamick Central School in Hudson, N.Y.

- Lucille Fay LeSueur, better known as actress Joan Crawford, was born in San Antonio. As a child, she moved with her mother to Lawton, Okla.

- Singer-actress Dale Evans was born in Uvalde but moved with her family to Arkansas as a teen.

- Famed criminal defense attorney Percy Foreman was born in Cold Springs. He quit school at age fifteen and later attended Staunton Military Academy in Virginia.

- Soul singer Barry White was born in Galveston but was raised in Los Angeles.

- Country singer Freddy Fender was born Baldemer Huerta in San Benito. He quit school in 1953 at age sixteen to join the U.S. Marines.

- Hall of Fame baseball player/ manager Frank Robinson was born in Beaumont but grew up in Oakland, California. He graduated from McClymonds High in Oakland.

- Paula Ragusa, later known as actress Paula Prentiss, was born in San Antonio. She graduated from Randolph Macon School in Virginia.

- Jimmy Demaret attended the old Houston North Side High before quitting school to become a golf pro in the late 1920s. He won several major golf championships.

Vocabulary

Prom — a formal dance given by a high school or college class

Extra Credit

- Sissy Spacek, Quitman (Homecoming Queen, Most Energetic)
- H. B. "Barefoot" Sanders, North Dallas (Best All-Round Boy)
- Stanley Marcus, Dallas Forest Avenue (Most Natural Boy)
- Phyllis George, Denton (First Period Office Assistant)
- Michael Martin Murphey, Dallas Adamson (winner, Law Essay Contest)

Quitman High School

- J. P. Richardson Jr., Beaumont (homeroom president)
- Jaclyn Smith, Houston Lamar (gym leader)
- Nolan Ryan, Alvin (Most Handsome)
- Matthew McConaughey, Longview (Most Handsome)
- Tom Landry, Mission (Cutest Boy)
- Ann O'Brien, Richardson (fifth place in State Rally for World)

- Linda Smith Ellerbee, Houston Lamar (gym leader)
- Jessica Simpson, Richardson Pearce (homecoming queen)
- Janis Joplin, Port Arthur Jefferson (Slide Rule Club)
- Don Baylor, Austin Stephen F. Austin (Sergeant-at-Arms)
- Dorothy Ann Willis, a.k.a. Ann Richards, Waco High (Girls Nation delegate)
- Barbara Jordan, Houston Wheatley (first place in National United Ushers

134

- Association, Zeta Phi Beta Girl of the Year)
- William P. Clements Jr., Highland Park (Senior Most Popular Boy)
- Charles "Tex" Watson, Farmersville (School Favorite)
- Larry Johnson, Dallas Skyline (Most Likely To Succeed)
- Jeri Lynn Mooney (Susan Howard), Marshall (UIL Best Actress)
- Van Cliburn, Kilgore (Most Ambitious)
- Jerry Faye Hall, North Mesquite (Most Likely to Succeed)
- Larry Gatlin, Odessa High (All State Choir)
- Laura Welch Bush, Midland Lee (Homecoming Queen nominee)
- Betty Buckley, Fort Worth Arlington Heights (Most Talented)
- Jack Mildren, Abilene Cooper (Mr. Cooper High School)
- Karen Parfitt Hughes, Dallas W. T. White (National Merit Letter of Commendation)
- Jeannie Stephenson (Jeannie C. Riley), Anson High (Most Popular Girl)
- Kay Bailey, LaMarque (Homecoming Queen, Miss LMHS)
- Walt Garrison, Lewisville (Most Handsome, Senior Class)
- Trini Lopez, Dallas Crozier Tech (Class Favorite)

Paris High School, circa 1950.

- Gene Stallings, Paris (Senior Favorite, Senior Who's Who)
- Davey O'Brien, Dallas Woodrow Wilson (Popularity Contest winner)
- Domingo Samudio, Dallas Crozier Tech (Wittiest)
- Kenneth Starr, San Antonio Houston (Most Likely to Succeed)

PVIL Holds Storied Place in History

From 1940 to 1967, the Prairie View Interscholastic League was the governing body for interscholastic competitions between public black high schools in Texas. The organization was originally called the Texas Interscholastic League of Colored Schools (TILCS). In 1967 and '68 most of the PVIL members integrated into the University Interscholastic League. The last PVIL championship game was held in 1969. In 1970 the UIL became the governing body for all public high school interscholastic activities in Texas. The original 21 schools in the PVIL in 1940 were: Marshall, Texarkana, Longview, Tyler, Kilgore, Paris, Dallas Lincoln, Dallas Washington, Ft. Worth Terrell, Wichita Falls Washington, Beaumont Charlton-Pollard, Port Arthur Lincoln, Galveston Central, Houston Washington, Houston Wheatley, Houston Yates, Waco Moore, Austin Anderson, San Antonio Wheatley, Victoria, and Corpus Christi Cole.

The Most Famous
(or Infamous) Reunion

Arguably the most famous (or infamous) high school reunion ever held in Texas was the 10-year reunion of Port Arthur Thomas Jefferson students in August of 1970. Janis Joplin, who by that time had earned fame as a rock/blues singer, was an outcast and rebel during her high school days. Apparently, her intentions in attending the reunion were to show up those former classmates who had been cruel to her.

Joplin announced her plans to attend the reunion during a television interview with Dick Cavett. During the interview, Joplin asked Cavett, "Would you like to go, man?" Cavett replied, "Well, Janis, I don't have that many friends in your high school class." To which she said, "I don't either, man," adding, "that's why I'm going." She went on to comment, "They laughed me out of class, out of town, and out of state, so I'm going home."

On the day of the reunion, Joplin held a press conference, where she was quizzed about her high school days. Suddenly, all the bad memories returned. On more than one occasion, Joplin lost her composure; her visible pain was terrible to see.

The reunion dinner was no better. After the dinner, when everyone's accomplishments were recognized, the master of ceremonies said, "Is there anything I've missed?" Someone responded, "Janis Joplin." There was scattered applause, Janis took a bow, and she was presented a gag gift (a tire) for having come the greatest distance. This lack of respect and recognition was crushing for Joplin. Within two months, she would be dead of a drug overdose.

Charlie's Texas Angels

One of the most popular television shows in the 1970s was *Charlie's Angels*, a sexy detective series. Two of the original three angels — Farrah Fawcett (Corpus Christi Ray) and Jaclyn Smith (Houston Lamar) — are Texas hotshots. The show's producer, Aaron Spelling, also graduated from high school in Texas (Dallas Forest Avenue). Fawcett played the role of Jill Munroe on the series. Meanwhile, Smith was cast as Kelly Garrett. The third angel, Sabrina Duncan, was played by actress Kate Jackson. Also starring in the show were David Doyle and John Forsythe (who played the never-seen character Charlie). The show was a consistent ratings success for the ABC network.

Alvin High

NOLAN RYAN
(1965)
Hall of Fame baseball
pitcher

Alvin High

KENT WALDREP
(1972)
College football player/
Advocate for Americans
with Disabilities Act

Beaumont Charlton-Pollard High

CHARLES SMITH
(1963)

BUBBA SMITH
Hall of Fame football
player

Beaumont French High

OAIL PHILLIPS
(1942)

"BUM" PHILLIPS
Pro football coach
Houston Oilers
New Orleans Saints

Beaumont Hebert High

JERRY LEVIAS
(1965)
First African-American
football star in the
Southwest Conference

Beaumont High

MILDRED DIDRIKSON

BABE DIDRIKSON
ZAHARIAS
Outstanding female
athlete

Beaumont High

JOHN TOWER
(1943)
U.S. senator

140

Beaumont High

J. P. RICHARDSON JR.
(1947)

THE BIG BOPPER
Disc jockey/recording
artist
"Chantilly Lace"

Beaumont South Park High

WOODARD RITTER
(1922)

"TEX" RITTER
Singing cowboy
"High Noon"

Beaumont South Park High

MARK CHESNUTT
Country musician

Corpus Christi Mary Carroll High

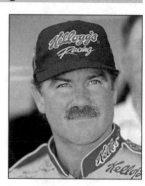

TERRY LABONTE
(1975)
NASCAR champion

Corpus Christi King High

BURT HOOTON
(1967)
Major League baseball
pitcher

Corpus Christi W. B. Ray High

FARRAH FAWCETT
(1965)
Actress
Charlie's Angels

Dickinson High

TRACY SCOGGINS
(1970)
Actress
*Babylon 5, Dynasty,
The Colbys, Lois & Clark*

Dickinson High

ANDRE WARE
(1986)
Heisman Trophy winner

Floresville High

JOHN CONNALLY
(1933)
Texas governor

143

Houston Bellaire High

RANDY QUAID
(1968)
Actor
The Last Detail,
National Lampoon
Vacation

Houston Bellaire High

DENNIS QUAID
(1972)
Actor
The Rookie,
The Right Stuff,
The Big Easy

Houston Jefferson Davis High

KENNY ROGERS
(1956)
Singer/musician
"The Gambler"

Houston Jesse H. Jones High

JOBETH WILLIAMS
Actress
Poltergeist,
Teachers

Houston Kinkaid School

GEORGE W. BUSH
U.S. president

Houston Mirabeau B. Lamar High

TOMMY TUNE
(1957)
Broadway dancer

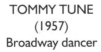

Houston Mirabeau B. Lamar High

MARK WHITE
(1958)
Texas governor

Houston Mirabeau B. Lamar High

LINDA SMITH
(1962)

LINDA ELLERBEE
TV journalist

Houston Mirabeau B. Lamar High

ELLEN SMITH
(1964)

JACLYN SMITH
Actress
Charlie's Angels

Houston Robert E. Lee High

BILLY GIBBONS
(1967)
Member of ZZ Top rock
group

Houston John H. Reagan High

RED ADAIR
Firefighter

Houston John H. Reagan High

MARY KAY WAGNER
(1935)

MARY KAY ASH
Cosmetics entrepreneur
Mary Kay Cosmetics

Houston John H. Reagan High

DAN RATHER
(1950)
TV journalist
CBS Evening News

Houston John H. Reagan High

ANTHONY FOYT

A. J. FOYT
Racecar driver
Indy 500 winner

Houston Sam Houston High

JACK VALENTI
(1937)
Presidential advisor to
Lyndon Johnson/Motion
Picture Association
president

Houston San Jacinto High

WALTER CRONKITE
(1933)
TV journalist
CBS Evening News

Houston San Jacinto High

DR. DENTON COOLEY
(1937)
Heart surgeon

Houston St. Thomas High

JACK BURKE JR.
(1940)
Pro golfer, Masters and
PGA champion

Houston St. Thomas High

DAVE MARR
(1950)
Pro golfer,
PGA champion

Houston Worthing High

MIKE SINGLETARY
(1977)
Hall of Fame professional
football player

Houston S. P. Waltrip High

SHELLEY DUVALL
(1967)
Actress
*The Shining,
Popeye*

Houston S. P. Waltrip High

PATRICK SWAYZE
(1971)
Actor
Dirty Dancing

Houston Phillis Wheatley High

BARBARA JORDAN
(1952)
Congresswoman

Houston Jack Yates High

PHYLICIA ALLEN
(1966)

**PHYLICIA ALLEN
RASHAD**
Actress
The Cosby Show

151

Katy High

CLINT BLACK
Country musician
"Killin' Time"

Kerrville Tivy High

DRAYTON MAHAFFEY
(1966)

JOHN MAHAFFEY
Professional golfer,
PGA Champion

Klein High

LYLE LOVETT
(1975)
Country musician

LaMarque High

KAY BAILEY
(1962)

KAY BAILEY
HUTCHISON
U.S. senator

Mission High

LLOYD BENTSEN
(1939)
U.S. senator

Mission High

TOM LANDRY
(1942)
Dallas Cowboys football
coach

Pearsall High

GEORGE STRAIT
(1970)
Country musician

Port Arthur Thomas Jefferson High

JANIS JOPLIN
(1960)
Rock/blues musician
"Me and Bobby McGee"

Port Arthur Thomas Jefferson High

JIMMY JOHNSON
(1961)
College/pro football
coach

Port Arthur Thomas Jefferson High

THOMAS HICKS
(1964)
Businessman/sports
team owner

Port Isabel High

RONNIE DUNN
(1971)
Member of
Brooks & Dunn
country music duo

High School Confidential

Rick Perry, Texas's 47th governor, is a 1969 graduate of Paint Creek School. Paint Creek is a small community located 60 miles north of Abilene. Perry played six-man football and basketball and ran track at the school, whose motto is "No Dream Too Tall for a School So Small." Perry's graduating class was comprised of thirteen students.

Rosenberg Lamar Consolidated High

BILLIE JOE THOMAS
(1959)

B. J. THOMAS
Pop/gospel musician

San Antonio Alamo Heights High

PONCE CRUSE
(1969)

HELOISE
Newspaper columnist

San Antonio Alamo Heights High

CHRISTOPHER
GEPPERT
(1969)

CHRISTOPHER CROSS
Grammy Award-winning
pop musician

San Antonio Central Catholic High

HENRY CISNEROS
(1964)
San Antonio mayor/HUD
Secretary

San Antonio Cole High

SHAQUILLE O'NEAL
(1990)
Pro basketball player

San Antonio Sam Houston High

KENNETH STARR
(1964)
Special Prosecutor
Whitewater investigation

157

San Antonio Southwest High

TY DETMER
(1990)
Heisman Trophy winner

San Antonio Thomas Jefferson High

HENRY GONZALEZ
(1934)
U.S. Congressman

San Antonio Thomas Jefferson High

KYLE ROTE
(1947)
Hall of Fame football
player

San Antonio Thomas Jefferson High

JIM LEHRER
TV journalist

San Antonio Thomas Jefferson High

TOMMY NOBIS
(1962)
Hall of Fame football
player

Santa Fe High

JOHNNY LEE
Country musician
"Lookin' for Love"

Spring Woods High

ROGER CLEMENS
(1979)
Major League baseball
pitcher/Cy
Young Award winner

Sugar Land High

KENNETH HALL
(1954)
Texas high school
football's
all-time leading rusher

Vidor High

TRACY BYRD
(1985)
Country musician
"Holdin' Heaven"
"The Keeper of the
Stars"

Vidor High

CLAY WALKER
(1987)
Country singer

Wharton High

HORTON FOOTE
(1932)
Screenwriter
To Kill A Mockingbird

High School Confidential

Renowned heart surgeon Dr. Denton Cooley (Houston San Jacinto High, '37) is a member of the Texas High School Basketball Hall of Fame.

Not Pictured:

Edna High
STEVE WILLIAMS
(1982)
STEVE AUSTIN
"STONE COLD" AUSTIN
Pro wrestler

Houston Heights High (Now Reagan High)
CLAUDE RAINS
Actor
The Invisible Man,
Mr. Smith Goes to Washington,
Casablanca

Houston John H. Reagan High
RICHARD HAYNES
"RACEHORSE" HAYNES
Criminal defense attorney

Houston Jack Yates High
DEBBIE ALLEN
(1968)
Actress
Fame

San Antonio Sam Houston High
DOUG SAHM
(1960)
Musician
Member of Sir Douglas
Quintet, Texas Tornadoes

162

Extra Credit Candids

Kay Bailey is crowned Homecoming Queen at LaMarque High School in 1961. Years later Kay Bailey Hutchison was elected to the United States Senate.

Sissy Spacek was elected Homecoming Queen at Quitman High School in 1967. Spacek became an award-winning actress, starring in such movies as *Carrie*, *Coal Miner's Daughter*, and *In the Bedroom*.

Plano High School student Greg Ray, center, works during an electronics class in the early 1980s. After graduation, Ray found the spotlight as a racecar driver.

Anson High School's band sweetheart and Most Popular Girl in 1964 was Jeanne Stephenson. In 1968 Stephenson, now known as Jeannie C. Riley, recorded a number one pop hit, "Harper Valley PTA."

Named Most Handsome at Longview High School in 1987 was Matthew McConaughey. Through 2002 McConaughey had appeared in 23 movies, including *The Newton Boys*, *A Time to Kill*, *Lone Star*, and *Angels in the Outfield*. He has made guest TV appearances on *King of the*

Front row, third from left, Karen Parfitt was an outstanding student in the mid-1970s at Dallas W. T. White High School. Karen Hughes served as a counselor to President George W. Bush.

Bill Paxton served as president of the Allied Youth Group at Fort Worth Arlington Heights in the 1970s. Today Paxton enjoys a successful acting career, appearing in such movies as *Twister* and *Titanic*.

"Mr. Cooper High School" in 1968 was Jack Mildren. Mildren was later elected lieutenant governor of Oklahoma.

Pictured in the 1950 Waco High yearbook is Dorothy Ann Willis. Ann Richards was elected governor of Texas in 1990.

165

Among the members of the Wink High School yearbook staff in the early 1950s was Roy Orbison (standing, second from right). Orbison established himself as a rock 'n' roll music pioneer, recording such hits as "Oh Pretty Woman," "Only the Lonely," and "Crying."

Bebes (Gene) Stallings, left, served as president of the Paris High School Future Farmers of America in the early 1950s. Stallings was an outstanding football coach, leading the University of Alabama to a national title and Texas A&M University to a Cotton Bowl win. Stallings also coached in the National Football League.

Voted Most Talented Girl at Fort Worth Arlington Heights in 1963 was future actress Betty Buckley. Buckley has appeared on TV, in the movies, and on Broadway.

Down Memory Lane: The Movies

Best Picture Year-by-Year

1927 – *Wings*

1929 – *The Broadway Melody*

1930 – *All Quiet on the Western Front*

1931 – *Cimarron*

1932 – *Grand Hotel*

1933 – *Cavalcade*

1934 – *It Happened One Night*

1935 – *Mutiny on the Bounty*

1936 – *The Great Ziegfeld*

1937 – *The Life of Emile Zola*

1938 – *You Can't Take It With You*

1939 – *Gone With the Wind*

1940 – *Rebecca*

1941 – *How Green Was My Valley*

1942 – *Mrs. Miniver*

1943 – *Casablanca*

1944 – *Going My Way*

1945 – *The Lost Weekend*

1946 – *The Best Years of Our Lives*

1947 – *Gentleman's Agreement*

1948 – *Hamlet*

1949 – *All the King's Men*

1950 – *All About Eve*

1951 – *An American in Paris*

1952 – *The Greatest Show on Earth*

1953 – *From Here to Eternity*

1954 – *On the Waterfront*

1955 – *Marty*

1956 – *Around the World in Eighty Days*

1957 – *The Bridge on the River Kwai*

1958 – *Gigi*

1959 – *Ben Hur*

1960 – *The Apartment*

1961 – *West Side Story*

1962 – *Lawrence of Arabia*

1963 – *Tom Jones*

1964 – *My Fair Lady*

1965 – *The Sound of Music*

1966 – *A Man for All Seasons*

1967 – *In the Heat of the Night*

1968 – *Oliver!*

1969 – *Midnight Cowboy*

1970 – *Patton*

1971 – *The French Connection*

1972 – *The Godfather*

1973 – *The Sting*

1974 – *The Godfather, Part II*

1975 – *One Flew Over the Cuckoo's Nest*

1976 – *Rocky*

1977 – *Annie Hall*

1978 – *The Deerhunter*

1979 – *Kramer vs. Kramer*

1980 – *Ordinary People*

1981 – *Chariots of Fire*

1982 – *Gandhi*

1983 – *Terms of Endearment*

1984 – *Amadeus*

1985 – *Out of Africa*

1986 – *Platoon*

1987 – *The Last Emperor*

1988 – *Rain Man*

1989 – *Driving Miss Daisy*

1990 – *Dances With Wolves*

1991 – *The Silence of the Lambs*

1992 – *Unforgiven*

1993 – *Schindler's List*

1994 – *Forrest Gump*

1995 – *Braveheart*

1996 – *The English Patient*

1997 – *Titanic*

1998 – *Shakespeare In Love*

1999 – *American Beauty*

2000 – *Gladiator*

2001 – *A Beautiful Mind*

Arlington Martin Yearbook Wins Accolades from Time

New York mayor Rudolph Giuliani was named person of the year by *Time* Magazine in 2002. The same magazine deemed Arlington Martin High School's yearbook the best in the country in 2002. A staff of 40 students produced the yearbook, which was titled, "4 Years in the Making." The yearbook chronicled the high school careers of Martin's first ninth-grade class.

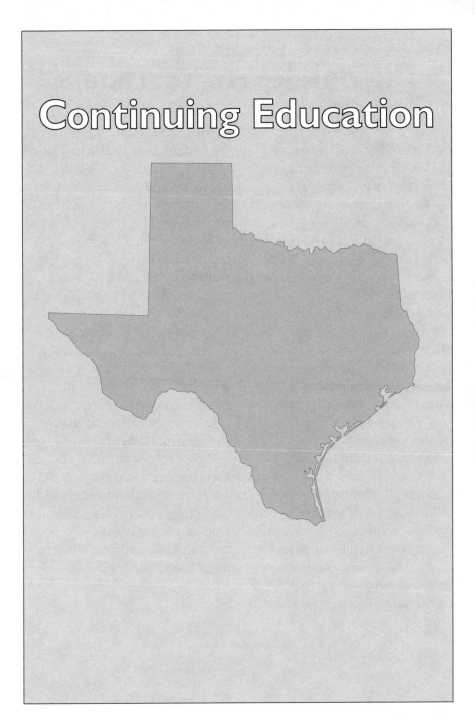

Continuing Education

The Business of Yearbooks

Two of the largest yearbook makers today are Jostens and Taylor Publishing Company.

Jostens was founded as a jewelry and watch repair company in 1897 in Owatonna, Minnesota. In 1900 the company expanded to manufacture emblems and awards for area schools. In 1906 company founder Otto Josten began making class rings. Jostens organized the American Yearbook Company in 1950 as a division to sell yearbooks throughout the United States. In 1969 Jostens moved its corporate headquarters from Owatonna to Minneapolis, Minnesota.

Today Jostens prints about 7 million copies of yearbooks each year for about 18,000 schools. It also produces class rings and graduation products, including caps and gowns, diplomas, graduation announcements, and accessories.

In 1923 H. C. and E. M. Taylor bought Star Engraving in Houston, Texas and began printing diplomas, invitations, and announcements and began producing class rings. (A few years later Bill Taylor joined the company as a sales representative.) In 1939 Taylor introduced offset lithography to yearbook printing. Taylor Engraving was reorganized in Dallas and began gradually to phase out the announcement and class ring business. In 1948 the company combined typesetting, printing, binding, and cover production under one roof to create a how-to book on yearbook production for students. To accommodate growth, the company purchased a 13-acre tract of land off Mockingbird Lane in Dallas to house its company headquarters in 1964.

Some Unusual Yearbook Names

Coushatta — Bonham HS
Svegit — Commerce HS
Warbonnet — Tuloso-Midway HS
Otyokwa — Ysleta HS
Planonian — Plano HS
Graffitti — Pleasanton HS
Roustabout — Price HS
Tepee — Seminole HS
Vandalite — Van HS
Stingaree — Victoria HS
The Gobbler — Cuero HS
The Crag — Decatur HS
The Brahma — East Bernard HS
Cicerone — Ennis HS

Lexington — Gonzales HS
Rimrock — Iraan HS
Aquila — Luling HS
Jolly Roger — Lytle HS
Paladin — Mayde Creek HS
El Paisano — Westlake HS
The Wolf Pack — Dallas Crozier Tech
The Plain View — Plainview
The Tiger Tale — LaMarque HS
Excalibur — Dallas Kimball
Sundial — Dallas Sunset
Melon Vine — Weatherford
Spindletop — Beaumont South Park

Largest Texas High School by Enrollment (2002)

Plano East — 5,481

Smallest Texas High School by Enrollment (2002)

Goree — 17

Presidents Who Attended Texas High Schools

Lyndon B. Johnson — Johnson City
George W. Bush — Houston Kinkaid

Miss Americas Who Attended Texas High Schools

1942 — Jo-Carroll Dennison — Tyler John Tyler
1971— Phyllis George — Denton High
1975 — Shirley Cothran — Denton High

Heisman Trophy Winners Who Attended Texas High Schools

1938 — Davey O'Brien — Dallas Woodrow Wilson
1948 — Doak Walker — Highland Park
1977 — Earl Campbell — Tyler John Tyler
1978 — Billy Sims — Hooks High
1987 — Tim Brown — Dallas Woodrow Wilson
1989 — Andre Ware — Dickinson High
1990 — Ty Detmer — San Antonio Southwest High

Seventeen Unusual Texas High School Mascots

Frost Polar Bears
Winters Blizzards
Groesbeck Goats
Hutto Hippos
El Campo Ricebirds
Palacios Sharks
Itasca Wampus Cats
Roscoe Plowboys
Springtown Porcupines
Progresso Red Ants

Knippa Purple Rock Crushers
Cuero Gobblers
Deer Park Deer
Fort Worth Polytechnic Parrots
Rotan Yellowhammers
Lake Worth Bullfrogs
Dallas Booker T. Washington
    School for the Visual and
    Performing Arts Pegasus

Ten Most Common Texas High School Mascots

Eagles
Bulldogs
Tigers
Panthers
Lions

Mustangs
Wildcats
Cougars
Indians
Pirates

Texas High Schools Where Elvis Presley Performed Concerts in 1955

Odessa High (3 times)
Midland High (3 times)
Gladewater High (twice)
Stamford High (twice)
Gaston High
Alpine High

DeKalb High
Breckenridge High
Seymour High
Conroe High
Port Arthur Woodrow Wilson
Junior High

Rock and Roll Hall of Fame Members Who Attended Texas High Schools

Buddy Holly (Lubbock High)
Roy Orbison (Wink High)
Janis Joplin (Port Arthur Jefferson High)

Eleven Texas High Schools Where Movies Were Filmed

Archer City High — *The Last Picture Show* (1970)

Elgin High — *Varsity Blues* (1999)

Georgetown High football stadium — *Varsity Blues* (1999)

Mesquite Horn High — *Slap Her, She's French* (2001)

Mesquite Poteet High — *Slap Her, She's French* (2001)

Richardson Lake Highlands High — *Cotton Candy* (1978)

San Antonio Alamo Heights High, San Antonio Thomas Jefferson High — *Johnny B. Good* (1987)

San Antonio Thomas Jefferson High — *High School* (1940)

The Colony High — *Slap Her, She's French* (2001)

Thorndale High — *The Rookie* (2002)

Vega School — *What Matters Most* (2000)

Lake Highlands High School

Seven Infamous People Who Attended Texas High Schools

Lee Harvey Oswald, accused assassin of President John F. Kennedy — Ft. Worth Arlington Heights

Richard Speck, convicted of murdering eight student nurses in Chicago — Dallas Crozier Tech

Kenneth McDuff, notorious Texas serial killer — Rosebud High

Charles "Tex" Watson, member of Charles Manson "family," involved in Tate-LaBianca murders — Farmersville High

David Koresh, leader of Branch Davidian cult — Garland

John Hinckley Jr., attempted to assassinate President Ronald Reagan — Highland Park High

Bonnie Parker, member of the notorious Bonnie & Clyde Gang — Dallas Bryan Street High

Note: With the exception of Watson and Hinckley, all of the above dropped out of school.

Top 40 Pop Songs about High School

"High School Confidential," Jerry Lee Lewis
(#21 on charts in 1958)
"High School U.S.A.," Tommy Facenda
(#28 in 1959)
"High School Dance," Sylvers
(#17 in 1977)

Three Hotshots Who Hosted The Tonight Show

Don Meredith
Kenny Rogers
John Denver

Eleven People Who Attended Texas High Schools and Later Changed Their Names

Virginia Katherine McMath — Ft. Worth Central High (Ginger Rogers)

Vera Jayne Peers — Highland Park High (Jayne Mansfield)

Baldemer Huerta — San Benito High (Freddy Fender)

Jeri Lynn Mooney — Marshall High (Susan Howard)

John Deutschendorf — Ft. Worth Arlington Heights (John Denver)

Patsy McClenny — Richardson Lake Highlands (Morgan Fairchild)

Christopher Geppert — San Antonio Alamo Heights (Christopher Cross)

Vernon Howell — Garland (David Koresh)

Vickie Hogan, Vickie Smith, Nikki Hogan, Nikki Hart — Mexia High (Anna Nicole Smith)

Neal McGaughey — Jacksonville High (Neal McCoy)

Ponce Cruse — San Antonio Alamo Heights (Heloise)

Three Texas High School Hotshots Known as "Tex"

Frederick Bean "Tex" Avery — North Dallas High (cartoonist)

Woodard "Tex" Ritter — Beaumont South Park High (singing cowboy)

Charles "Tex" Watson — Farmersville High (convicted murderer)

Twelve Hotshots Who Attended Private High Schools

George W. Bush — Houston Kinkaid

Steve Miller — St. Mark's School of Texas

Boz Scaggs — St. Mark's School of Texas

Tommy Lee Jones — St. Mark's School of Texas

Lance Armstrong — Bending Oaks Academy

John Hillerman — Denison St. Xavier's

Patricia Richardson — The Hockaday School

Lisa Loeb — The Hockaday School

Brenda Vacarro — The Hockaday School

Henry Cisneros — San Antonio Central Catholic

Jack Burke Jr. — Houston St. Thomas

Dave Marr — Houston St. Thomas

Nine "Junior" Hotshots

G. A. Moore Jr.

Roy Hargrove Jr.

John Hinckley Jr.

Raymond Berry Jr.

William Clements Jr.

Miller Barber Jr.

Drayton McLane Jr.

J. P. Richardson Jr.

Jack Burke Jr.

Texas High School Hotshots Who Were Classmates

Dallas Skyline High — Larry Johnson and Michael Johnson

Dallas Adamson High — B. W. Stevenson, Michael Martin

Murphey, and Ray Wylie Hubbard

Houston Lamar High — Tommy Tune and Mark White

St. Mark's School of Texas —
Boz Scaggs and Steve Miller
Texarkana Texas High — H.
Ross Perot and Miller Barber
Dallas Crozier Tech — Trini
Lopez and Domingo Samudio
Stamford High — Charles
Stenholm and Charles Coody
Port Arthur Thomas Jefferson
— Jimmy Johnson and Janis
Joplin
Houston Lamar — Linda
Ellerbee and Jaclyn Smith
Highland Park — Bobby Layne
and Doak Walker
Dallas Thomas Jefferson —
Brenda Vacarro and Michael
Nesmith

Booker T. Washington School
for the Visual and Per-
forming Arts — Erykah
Badu and Roy Hargrove Jr.
Fort Worth Arlington Heights
— T. Cullen Davis and
Thomas Thompson
Fort Worth Arlington Heights
— John Denver and Betty
Buckley
Fort Worth Paschal — Dan
Jenkins and Alan Bean
San Antonio Alamo Heights —
Christopher Cross and Ponce
Cruse (Heloise)
Vidor — Tracy Byrd and Clay
Walker

Six Hotshots Known by Their Initials

Y. A. Tittle (Yelberton
Abraham)
B. J. Thomas (Billie Joe)
A. J. Foyt (Anthony Joseph)

G. A. Moore (Gene Autry)
B. W. Stevenson (Louis
"Buckwheat")
J. P. Richardson Jr. (Jiles P.)

Nine Hotshot Transfer Students

George W. Bush, transferred
from Houston Kinkaid to
Phillips Academy
Tommy Lee Jones, San Saba to
St. Mark's School of Texas

Boz Scaggs, Plano High to St.
Mark's School of Texas
Steve Miller, St. Mark's School
of Texas to Dallas Woodrow
Wilson

Lance Armstrong, Plano East Senior High to Bending Oaks Academy

Brenda Vacarro, Hockaday School for Girls to Dallas Thomas Jefferson

Jim Lehrer, Beaumont French to San Antonio Jefferson

Tex Ritter, Carthage to Beaumont South Park

Thomas "Hollywood" Henderson, Austin Anderson to Oklahoma City Douglas

Ten Honorary Texas Hotshots

George Bush
Roger Staubach
Jerry Jeff Walker
Ray Benson
Tex Schramm

Abe Lemons
Bob Knight
Chuck Norris
Darrell Royal
Mickey Mantle

Nine Hotshots You Know by Their Nickname

"Dandy" Don Meredith
Thomas "Hollywood" Henderson
Bill "Boz" Scaggs
Richard "Racehorse" Haynes
"Stevie Guitar" Miller

Brian "Boz" Bosworth
Dennis "Worm" Rodman
Miller "Mr. X" Barber
William Forrest "Blackie" Sherrod

Three Hotshot Singers Who Dropped Out of School But Later Earned Their GED

LeAnn Rimes
Selena
Jessica Simpson

Eleven Hotshot Schools That Are No Longer in Existence

Dallas N. R. Crozier Tech — Trini Lopez, Domingo Samudio, Richard Speck

Denison St. Xavier's Academy — John Hillerman

Grand Prairie Dal-Worth High — Charley Taylor

Mineola McFarland School — Willie Brown

Temple Dunbar High — Joe Greene

Beaumont Charlton-Pollard — Bubba Smith

Beaumont French — Bum Phillips

Beaumont Hebert — Jerry Levias

Beaumont High — Babe Didrikson, John Tower, J. P. Richardson Jr.

Beaumont South Park — Tex Ritter, Mark Chesnutt

Sugar Land High — Kenneth Hall

Three Hotshots Who Quit School to Join the Military

Johnny Lee — Santa Fe High — Marines
Freddy Fender — San Benito — Marines
Jimmy Dean — Plainview High — Merchant Marines

Songs Recorded by Don Meredith

"Them That Ain't Got It Can't Lose"
"Traveling Man"

The Band Names of Hotshots in High School

The Marksmen — Boz Scaggs and Steve Miller — St. Mark's School of Texas
The Roadrunners — Johnny Lee — Santa Fe High
Wink Westerners — Roy Orbison — Wink High
The Triumphs — B. J. Thomas — Lamar Consolidated

The Speeds, Felicity — Don Henley — Linden-Kildare High
The Coachmen, Moving Sidewalks — Billy Gibbons — Houston Lee
Blackbird — Stevie Ray Vaughan — Dallas Kimball
Us — B. W. Stevenson — Dallas Adamson

Archer City High School

Advertising

Aliceson Wallace, Matthew McConaughey and Lucy Henderson

SYLVAN LEARNING CENTER

"Where the gang meets"

BOSTICK'S RESTAURANT

Sandra Day trys to ask Beverly Tomlin, who is feeding her face, how the rolls are, as Dick Bunger finds one with a 'lot' of icing on it. But they all come to the conclusion that MEADS do have fine rolls and bread.

MEADS 'FINE' BREAD

matthew mcconaughey   rolu bindler

donn bindler interiors
1100 judson road suite 640

Autographs

Autographs

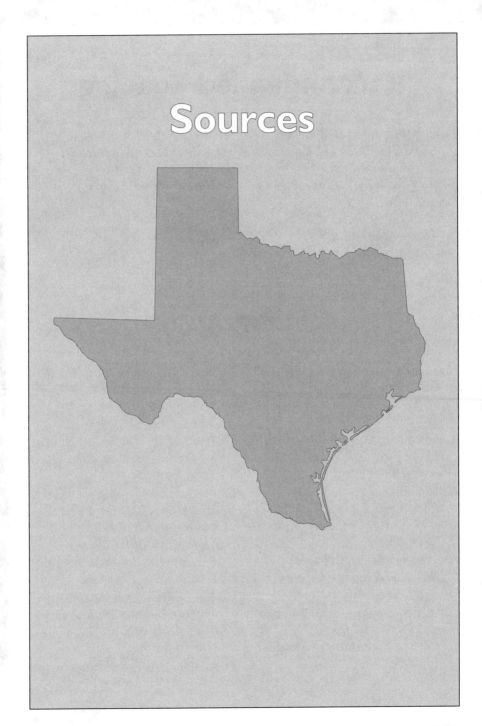

Sources

Recommended Reading

Blumenthal, John. *Hollywood High: The History of America's Most Famous Public School.* New York: Ballantine, 1988.

Greene, Bob. *Be True to Your School: A Diary of 1964.* New York: Athenium, 1987.

Medved, Michael, and David Wallechinsky. *What Really Happened to the Class of '65?* New York: Ballantine, 1976.

Bibliography

Abrams, Rick. "Rock Stars Relive Good Times at St. Mark's." *Dallas Morning News*, 30 Oct. 1983.

Adams, Leon. *Larry Hagman: A Biography.* New York: St. Martin's, 1987.

Adler, Bill, and Bill Adler, Jr., eds. *Ross Perot: An American Maverick Speaks Out.* New York: Carol, 1994.

Alexander, Charles C. *Rogers Hornsby: A Biography.* New York: Holt, 1995.

Allen, Bob. *George Jones: The Life and Times of a Honky Tonk Legend.* Tom Doherty Assoc., 1995.

Amburn, Ellis. *Dark Star: The Roy Orbison Story.* New York: Carol Publishing, 1990.

Armstrong, Lance, with Sally Jenkins. *It's Not About the Bike: My Journey Back to Life.* New York: Putnam, 2000.

Banks, Ernie and Jim Enright. *Mister Cub.* Chicago: Follett Publishing Co., 1971.

Barta, Carolyn. *Bill Clements, Texan to His Toenails.* Austin: Eakin, 1986.

Baylor, Don, with Claire Smith. *Nothing But the Truth: A Baseball Life.* New York: St. Martin's, 1989.

Bego, Mark. *George Strait: The Story of Country's Living*

Legend. New York: Kensington Books, 1997.

_____. *Ice Ice Ice: The Extraordinary Vanilla Ice Story*. New York: Dell, 1991.

Blayney, David. *Sharp Dressed Men: ZZ Top Behind the Scenes from Blues to Boogie to Beards*. New York: Hyperion, 1994.

Blumenthal, John. *Hollywood High: The History of America's Most Famous School*. New York: Ballantine, 1988.

Bosworth, Brian, with Rick Reilly. *The Boz: Confessions of a Modern Anti-Hero*. New York: Charter, 1989.

Bracken, Dorothy Kendall, as told by Doak Walker. *Doak Walker: Three-Time All-American*. Austin: Steck, 1950.

Breo, Dennis, and William J. Martin. *The Crime of the Century: Richard Speck and the Murder of Eight Nurses*. New York: Bantam, 1993.

Burnett, Carol. *One More Time: A Memoir*. New York: Random House, 1986.

Butts, J. Lee. *Texas Bad Girls: Hussies, Harlots, and Horse Thieves*. Plano: Republic of Texas Press, 2001.

Calhoun, Fryar. "Hi! I'm Jimmy Dean and I'd Like You to Try My Pure Pork Sausage." *Texas Monthly*. Aug. 1983.

Campbell, Dave. *Texas Football Magazine*.

Carpenter, Liz. *Getting Better All the Time*. New York: Simon & Schuster, 1987.

Cartwright, Gary. *Texas Justice: The Murder Trials of T. Cullen Davis*. New York: Pocket, 1979.

Casad, Dede Weldon. *Texans Behind the News: Texas Journalists of the 20th Century*. Austin: Eakin, 2000.

Cashion, Ty. *Pigskin Pulpit: A Social History of Texas High School Football Coaches*. Austin: Texas State Historical Assn., 1998.

Clark, J. Brent. *Third Down & Forever: Joe Don Looney & the Rise & Fall of an American Hero*. New York: St. Martin's, 1993.

Connally, John, with Mickey Herskowitz. *In History's Shadow: An American Odyssey*. New York: Hyperion, 1993.

Crenshaw, Ben, and Melanie Hauser. *A Feel for the Game: To Brookline and Back*. New York: Doubleday, 2001.

De Laet, Dianne Tittle. *Giants & Heroes: A Daughter's Memories of Y. A. Tittle*. South Royalton, Vt.: Steerforth Press, 1995.

Denver, John, with Arthur Tobier. *Take Me Home: An*

Autobiography. New York: Harmony Books, 1994.

Diehl, Kemper, and Jan Jarboe. *Cisneros: Portrait of a New American*. San Antonio: Corona, 1985.

Echols, Alice. *Scars of Sweet Paradise: The Life and Times of Janis Joplin*. New York: Holt, 1999.

Eliot, Marc. *To the Limit: The Untold Story of The Eagles*. Boston: Little, Brown, 1998.

Foreman, George, with Joel Engel. *By George: The Autobiography of George Foreman*. New York: Villard Books, 1995.

Foyt, A. J., with William Neely. *A. J.* New York: Times Books, 1983.

Friedman, Kinky. *Guide to Texas Etiquette: Or How to Get to Heaven or Hell Without Going Through Dallas-Fort Worth*. New York: Harper, 2001.

Fry, Hayden, with George Wine. *Hayden Fry: A High Porch Picnic*. Champaign, Ill: Sports Publishing, 1997.

Garrison, Walt, with John Tullius. *Once A Cowboy*. New York: Random, 1988.

Gatlin, Larry, with Jeff Lenburg. *All the Gold in California and Other People, Places and Things*. Nashville: Thomas Nelson, 1990.

Gholson, Nick. *Hail to Our Colors: A Complete History of Coyote Football*. Wichita Falls: 2000.

Goldrosen, John. *The Buddy Holly Story*. New York: Quick Fox, 1979.

Graham, Don. *No Name on the Bullet: A Biography of Audie Murphy*. New York: Viking, 1989.

Gray, Michael, and Roger Osborne. *The Elvis Atlas*. New York: Holt, 1996.

Grimsley, Will. *Football: The Greatest Moments in the Southwest Conference*. Boston: Little, Brown, 1968.

Hagman, Larry, with Todd Gold. *Hello Darlin': Tall and Absolutely True Tales About My Life*. New York: Simon, 2001.

Hall, Jerry, with Christopher Hemphill. *Jerry Hall: Tall Tales*. New York: Pocket, 1985.

Hamm, Mia, with Aaron Heifetz. *Go for the Goal*. New York: Harper-Collins, 1999.

Hargrove, Sharon, and Richard Hauer Costa. *Safe At Home: A Baseball Wife's Story*. College Station: Texas A&M UP, 1989.

Hawkins, John. *Texas Cheerleaders: The Spirit of America*. New York: St. Martin's, 1991.

Henderson, Thomas, and Peter Knobler. *Out of Control:*

Confessions of an NFL Casualty. New York: Pocket, 1987.

Hopwood, Thomas Milton. *Great Texans in Sports*. Ft. Worth: Hopwood Productions, 1975.

James, Doug. *Walter Cronkite: His Life and Times*. Brentwood: J. M. Press, 1991.

Jennings, Waylon, with Lenny Kaye. *Waylon: An Autobiography*. New York: Warner Books, 1996.

Johnson, Jimmy, as told to Ed Hinton. *Turning the Thing Around: Pulling America's Team Out of the Dumps and Myself Out of the Doghouse*. New York: Hyperion, 1993.

Johnson, Michael. *Slaying the Dragon: How to Turn Your Small Steps to Great Feats*. New York: Harper-Collins, 1996.

Johnson, William Oscar and Nancy P. Williamson. *Whatta-Gal: The Babe Didrikson Story*. Boston: Little, Brown & Co., 1975.

Jordan, Barbara, and Shelby Hearon. *Barbara Jordan, A Self-Portrait*. Garden City: Doubleday, 1979.

Jostens, Inc. *History Worth Repeating: A Chronology of School Yearbooks*. Winston-Salem, NC: Jostens Printing & Publishing Division, 1996.

Kaplan, Lincoln. *The Insanity Defense and the Trial of John W. Hinckley Jr.* Boston: D. R. Godine, 1984.

Keyes, Ralph. *Is There Life After High School?* Boston: Little, Brown, 1976.

King, Greg. *Sharon Tate and the Manson Murders*. New York: Barricade, 2000.

Landry, Tom, and Gregg Lewis. *Tom Landry: An Autobiography*. New York: Zondervan, 1990.

Lavergne, Gary M. *Bad Boy: The Murderous Life of Kenneth Allen McDuff*. New York: St. Martin's, 2001.

Lee, Johnny, with Randy Wyles. *Lookin' for Love*. Austin: Diamond Books, 1989.

Martin, Mary. *My Heart Belongs*. New York: Morrow, 1976.

McCally, Regina Walker. *The Secret of Mojo: The Story of the Odessa, Texas Permian High School Football Team*. Ft. Worth: R. W. McCally, 1986.

McMurray, Bill. *Texas High School Football*. South Bend: Icarus, 1985.

Meat Loaf, with David Dalton. *To Hell and Back: An Autobiography*. New York: Regan Books, 1999.

Miller, Merle. *Lyndon: An Oral Biography*. New York: G. P. Putnam's Sons, 1980.

Minutaglio, Bill. *First Son: George W. Bush and the Bush Family Dynasty*. New York: Random House, 1999.

Montgomery, Ruth. *Mrs. LBJ*. New York: Holt, Rinehart, 1964.

Nelson, Byron. *How I Played the Game: An Autobiography*. Dallas: Taylor, 1993.

Nelson, Willie, with Bud Shrake. *Willie, An Autobiography*. New York: Simon & Schuster, 1988.

Oberst, Stanley and Lori Torrance. *Elvis in Texas: The Undiscovered King 1954-1958*. Plano: Republic of Texas Press, 2002.

O'Neal, Bill. *Tex Ritter, America's Most Beloved Cowboy*. Austin: Eakin Press, 1998.

Oswald, Robert L., with Myrick and Barbara Land. *Lee, A Portrait of Lee Harvey Oswald By His Brother*. New York: Coward-McCann, 1967.

Patoski, Joe Nick. *Selena: Como La Flor*. Boston: Little, Brown, 1995.

Patoski, Joe Nick and Bill Crawford. *Stevie Ray Vaughan: Caught in the Crossfire*. Boston: Little, Brown, 1993.

Pennington, Richard. *Breaking the Ice: The Racial Integration of Southwest Conference Football*.

Jefferson, N.C.: McFarland, 1987.

Phillips, O. A. "Bum" and Ray Buck. *He Ain't No Bum*. Virginia Beach: Jordan, 1979.

Rather, Dan, with Peter Wyden. *I Remember*. Boston: Little, Brown & Co., 1991.

Ratliff, Harold V. *Autumn's Mightiest Legions: History of Texas Schoolboy Football*. Waco: Texian, 1963.

Ratliff, Harold V. *Texas Schoolboy Football: Champions in Action*. Austin: University Interscholastic League, 1972.

Reavis, Dick. *Ashes of Waco: An Investigation*. New York: Simon, 1995.

Reich, Howard. *Van Cliburn*. Nashville: T. Nelson, 1993.

Reid, Jan. *Vain Glory*. Fredericksburg: Shearer, 1986.

Reynolds, Debbie, with David Patrick Columbia. *Debbie — My Life*. New York: Pocket, 1989.

Rodman, Dennis, Pat Rich, Alan Steinberg. *Rebound: The Dennis Rodman Story*. New York: Crown, 1994.

Rogers, Ginger. *My Story*. New York: Harper-Collins, 1991.

Sampson, Curt. *Hogan*. Nashville: Rutledge Hill, 1996.

Saxton, Martha. *Jayne Mansfield and the American Fifties*.

Boston: Houghton Mifflin, 1975.

Schiebel, Walter J. E. *Education in Dallas: Ninety-Two Years of History*. Dallas: Taylor, 1966.

Singerman, Philip. *An American Hero: The Red Adair Story*. Boston: Little, 1990.

Smith, Liz. *Natural Blonde*. New York: Hyperion, 2000.

St. John, Bob. *Heart of a Lion: The Wild and Woolly Life of Bobby Layne*. Dallas: Taylor, 1991.

Stowers, Carlton. *Friday Night Heroes: Texas High School Football, Glory at the Goal Line*: Austin: Eakin, 1983.

Taylor Publishing Co. company brochure.

Thomas, B. J. *Home Where I Belong*. Waco: Word Books, 1978.

Tips, Kern. *Football Texas Style*: *An Illustrated History of the Southwest Conference*. Garden City: Doubleday, 1964.

Todd, Ed. "President? Young George W. Bush Just Wanted to Play Baseball." *Midland Reporter-Telegram*.

Townsend, Charles R. *San Antonio Rose: The Life and Music of Bob Wills*. Chicago: Univ. of Ill. Press, 1976.

Trevino, Lee, and Sam Blair. *They Call Me Super Mex*. New York: Random, 1982.

Truman State University. *Echo Yearbook*. Kirksville, Mo.

Tucker, Tanya, and Patsi B. Cox. *Nickel Dreams: My Life*. New York: Hyperion, 1997.

Watson, Tex, as told to Chaplain Ray. *Will You Die For Me?* Old Tappan, N.J.: Fleming H. Revell, 1978.

Whitburn, Joel. *The Billboard Book of Top 40 Hits*. New York: Billboard, 1985.

_____. *The Billboard Book of Top 40 Country Hits*. New York: Billboard, 1996.

Wood, Gordon, as told to John Carver. *Coach of the Century*. Dallas: Hard Times Cattle, 2001.

Other Sources

Austin Public Library
Dallas Public Library
Denison Public Library

Denton Public Library
Sherman Public Library

Internet Websites

Famous Texans
www.famoustexans.com
The Handbook of Texas Online
www.tsha-utexas.edu
Jostens
www.jostens.com
Notable Native Texans
www.texascooking.com
Pigskin Prep
www.allsports.com

San Antonio Convention and
Visitors Bureau
www.sanantoniocvb.com
The Star Archive
www.stararchive.com
The Texas State Library and
Archives Commission
www.tsl.state.tx.us
Taylor Publishing Company
www.taylorpub.com
University Interscholastic League
www.uil.utexas.edu

Photo Credits

High School Yearbooks

Abbott
Abilene Cooper
Alvin
Anson
Arp
Austin Stephen F. Austin
Austin McCallum
Beaumont
Beaumont Hebert
Beaumont South Park

Belton
Brownfield
Cameron Yoe
Dallas Adamson
Dallas Crozier Tech
Dallas Forest Avenue
Dallas Jefferson
Dallas Pinkston
Dallas Skyline
Dallas South Oak Cliff

Dallas Washington for the Visual
and Performing Arts
Dallas Wilson
Denison St. Xavier's
Denton
Dickinson
Farmersville
Fort Stockton
Fort Worth Arlington Heights
Fort Worth Paschal
Highland Park
Hillsboro
Hooks
Houston Bellaire
Houston Davis
Houston Heights
Houston Jones
Houston Lamar
Houston Lee
Houston Reagan
Houston Sam Houston
Houston San Jacinto
Houston Waltrip
Houston Wheatley
Houston Yates
Jacksonville
Johnson City
Kerrville Tivy
Kilgore
LaMarque
Lewisville
Longview

Lubbock
Lubbock Monterey
Marshall
Midland Lee
North Dallas
Paris
Pilot Point
Plano
Port Arthur Jefferson
Port Isabel
Quitman
Richardson
Richardson Lake Highlands
Rosenberg Lamar Consolidated
San Angelo
San Antonio Alamo Heights
San Antonio Houston
San Antonio Jefferson
San Antonio Southwest
Santa Fe
Snyder
Spring Woods
Stamford
Stephenville
Sulphur Springs
Texarkana Texas
Tyler Lee
Vidor
Waco
Weatherford
Wharton
Wink

Other Photo Credits

Austin History Center, Austin Public Library

Author's collection

Baltimore Orioles Baseball Club

Baylor University Sports Information Department

Buena Vista Television

Chicago Cubs Baseball Club

Dallas Cowboys Football Club

Dallas Morning News: Michael Ainsworth, Nancy Lee Andrews, Russell Bronson, Evans Caglege, Nan Coulter, Louis DeLuca, John Freilich, Chris Hamilton, Ariane Kadoch-Swisa, Joe Laird, Paula Nelson, Huy Nguyen, Carol Powers, Richard Pruitt, Mona Reeder, John Rhodes, Kim Ritzenthaler, Erich Schlegel, William Snyder, Jan Sonnenmair, Joseph Victor Stefanchik, Cindy Yamanaka, Irwin Thompson, David Woo.

Dallas Public Library

Denton Public Library

Detroit Lions Football Club

Disney

Fulbright & Jaworski

Grevy Photography

Herald Democrat Photo Archives

Houston Astros Baseball Club

Houston Comets Women's Basketball Team

Houston St. Thomas Archives

KILT Radio

Los Angeles Lakers Basketball Team

Oakland Raiders Football Club

Office of the Governor of Texas

Ronnie Perry's collection

Professional Golfers' Association Tour

Simon & Schuster

Southern Methodist University Sports Information Department

Summer Pierce

Texas A&M Sports Information Department

Texas Christian University – Mary Couts Burnett Library – Jim Wright

CollectionTexas Rangers Baseball Club

Texas Rehabilitation Commission

Texas Sounds

Texas Sports Hall of Fame

Texas Tech Sports Information Department

University of Texas Sports Information Department

University of North Texas Sports Information Department

Vanguard Records

Warner Brothers

Dr. Billy Wilbanks

Index by Person

A

Adair, Red, 147
Allen, Debbie, 162
Anderson, Donny, 27
Armstrong, Lance, 56
Ash, Mary Kay, 147
Austin, Steve, 162
Avery, Tex, 61

B

Badu, Erykah, 65
Baker, Joe Don, 122
Banks, Ernie, 64
Barber, Miller, 104
Baugh, Sammy, 27
Baylor, Don, 118
Bean, Alan, 71
Bentsen, Lloyd, 153
Berry, Raymond, 102
Black, Clint, 152
Blocker, Dan, 29
Boothe, Powers, 26
Bosworth, Brian, 75
Brickell, Edie, 64
Brown, Tim, 66
Brown, Willie, 101
Buckley, Betty, 69
Bullock, Bob, 119
Burke, Jack Jr., 149
Bush, George W., 145
Bush, Laura, 22
Byrd, Tracy, 160

C

Campbell, Earl, 105

Carpenter, Liz, 117
Cash, Norm, 25
Chesnutt, Mark, 141
Cisneros, Henry, 157
Clemens, Roger, 160
Clements, William P. Jr., 72
Cliburn, Van, 98
Connally, John, 143
Coody, Charles, 26
Cooley, Dr. Denton, 149
Corbin, Barry, 22
Cothran, Shirley, 67
Crenshaw, Ben, 118
Cronkite, Walter, 149
Cross, Christopher, 156

D

Davis, Mac, 21
Davis, T. Cullen, 79
Dean, Jimmy, 24
Dennison, Jo-Carroll, 105
Denver, John, 68
Detmer, Ty, 158
Duncan, Sandy, 104
Dunn, Ronnie, 155
Duvall, Shelley, 150

E

Ellerbee, Linda, 146

F

Fairchild, Morgan, 77
Fawcett, Farrah, 142
Foote, Horton, 161
Foxx, Jamie, 103

Foyt, A. J., 148
Fry, Hayden, 23

G
Garrison, Walt, 75
Gatlin, Larry, 23
George, Phyllis, 67
Gibbons, Billy, 147
Gonzalez, Henry, 158
Greene, Joe, 121
Gregg, Forrest, 103
Guldahl, Ralph, 65

H
Hagman, Larry, 78
Hall, Jerry, 75
Hall, Kenneth, 160
Hamm, Mia, 28
Hargrove, Mike, 24
Hargrove, Roy Jr., 64
Harmon, Angie, 74
Haynes, Richard "Racehorse," 162
Heloise, 156
Henderson, Thomas, 117
Henley, Don, 99
Hicks, Tom, 155
Hillerman, John, 67
Hinckley, John Jr., 73
Hogan, Ben, 69
Holly, Buddy, 21
Hooton, Burt, 142
Hornsby, Rogers, 70
Howard, Susan, 101
Hubbard, Ray Wylie, 58
Hughes, Karen, 65
Hutchison, Kay Bailey, 153

J
January, Don, 63
Jaworski, Leon, 121

Jenkins, Dan, 71
Jennings, Waylon, 29
Johnson, Jimmy, 154
Johnson, Lady Bird, 100
Johnson, Larry, 63
Johnson, Lyndon B., 120
Johnson, Michael, 62
Jones, Johnny, 120
Jones, Tommy Lee, 78
Joplin, Janis, 154
Jordan, Barbara, 151

K
King, Larry L., 29
Kite, Tom, 118

L
LaBonte, Terry, 142
Landry, Tom, 153
Lane, Dick, 122
Layne, Bobby, 72
Lee, Johnny, 159
Lehrer, Jim, 159
Leonard, Justin, 77
Levias, Jerry, 140
Lewis, Guy, 97
Lilly, Bob, 28
Loeb, Lisa, 74
Looney, Joe Don, 71
Lopez, Trini, 58
Lovett, Lyle, 152

M
Mahaffey, John, 152
Maines, Natalie, 22
Mansfield, Jayne, 73
Marcus, Stanley, 59
Marr, Dave, 150
Martin, Mary, 79
Matson, Randy, 24

McConaughey, Matthew, 99
McCoy, Neal, 98
McLane, Drayton Jr., 119
McMurtry, Larry, 20
Meat Loaf, 61
Meredith, Don, 101
Mildren, Jack, 19
Miller, Steve, 66
Moore, G. A., 76
Moyers, Bill, 100
Murphey, Michael Martin, 57

N

Nelson, Willie, 117
Nesmith, Michael 60
Nobis, Tommy, 159

O

O'Brien, Davey, 66
O'Connor, Sandra Day, 20
O'Neal, Shaquille, 157
Orbison, Roy, 28
Oswald, Lee Harvey, 68

P

Parker, Fess, 25
Parnell, Lee Roy, 27
Paxton, Bill, 69
Perot, Ross, 104
Perry, Rick, 23
Phillips, Bum, 139
Price, Ray, 57

Q

Quaid, Dennis, 144
Quaid, Randy, 144

R

Rains, Claude, 162
Rashad, Phylicia, 151

Rather, Dan, 148
Ray, Greg, 76
Reeves, Jim, 97
Rice, Anne, 76
Richards, Ann, 122
Richardson, J. P. Jr., 141
Richardson, Patricia, 74
Riley, Jeannie C., 19
Ritter, Tex, 141
Rodman, Dennis, 63
Rogers, Ginger, 79
Rogers, Kenny, 144
Rote, Kyle, 158
Rutherford, Johnny, 70
Ryan, Nolan, 138

S

Sahm, Doug, 162
Samudio, Domingo, 59
Sanders, Barefoot, 62
Scaggs, Boz, 77
Scoggins, Tracy, 143
Sheridan, Ann, 79
Sherrod, Blackie, 119
Sims, Billy, 97
Singletary, Mike, 150
Smith, Anna Nicole, 120
Smith, Bubba, 139
Smith, Jaclyn, 146
Smith, Liz, 70
Spacek, Sissy, 103
Spelling, Aaron, 60
Stallings, Gene, 102
Starr, Kenneth, 157
Stenholm, Charles, 26
Stevenson, B. W., 58
Strait, George, 154
Swayze, Patrick, 151
Swoopes, Sheryl, 20

T
Taylor, Charley, 72
Taylor, Regina, 62
Thomas, B. J., 156
Thompson, Thomas, 79
Tittle, Y. A., 100
Tower, John, 140
Tune, Tommy, 145

V
Vacarro, Brenda, 60
Valenti, Jack, 148
Vanilla Ice, 56
Vaughan, Stevie Ray, 61

W
Waldrep, Kent, 139

Walker, Clay, 161
Walker, Doak, 73
Ware, Andre, 143
Watson, Charles "Tex," 68
White, Mark, 146
Williams, Clayton, 21
Williams, Jo Beth, 145
Womack, Lee Ann, 98
Wood, Gordon, 19
Wright, Jim, 57

Y
Yarborough, Ralph, 105

Z
Zaharias, Babe Didrikson, 140

Index by High School

A
Abbott, 117
Abilene Cooper, 19
Abilene Wylie, 19
Alvin, 138, 139
Anson, 19
Archer City, 20
Arp, 97
Austin L. C. Anderson, 117, 122
Austin S. F. Austin, 117, 118
Austin McCallum, 118

B
Beaumont, 140, 141
Beaumont Charlton-Pollard, 139
Beaumont French, 139
Beaumont Hebert, 140
Beaumont South Park, 141
Belton, 119
Bending Oaks Academy, 56
Brownfield, 20

C
Cameron Yoe, 119
Carrollton R. L. Turner, 56
Carthage, 97
Corpus Christi Carroll, 142
Corpus Christi King, 142
Corpus Christi Ray, 142

D
Dallas Adamson, 57, 58
Dallas Crozier Tech, 58, 59
Dallas Forest Avenue, 59, 60
Dallas Jefferson, 60, 61

Dallas Kimball, 61
Dallas Pinkston, 62
Dallas Skyline, 62, 63
Dallas South Oak Cliff, 63
Dallas Sunset, 63
Dallas Washington, 64
Dallas Washington for the Visual and Performing Arts, 64, 65
Dallas White, 65
Dallas Wilson, 65, 66
Denison St. Xavier's Academy, 67
Denton, 67, 79
Dickinson, 143

E
Edna, 162
El Paso Austin, 20

F
Farmersville, 68
Floresville, 143
Fort Stockton, 21
Fort Worth Arlington Heights, 68, 69, 79
Fort Worth Central, 69, 79
Fort Worth North Side, 70
Fort Worth Paschal 70, 71

G
Grand Prairie Dal-Worth, 72
Groesbeck, 122

H
Highland Park, 72, 73, 74
Hillsboro, 119

Hockaday, 74
Hooks, 97
Houston Bellaire, 144
Houston Davis, 144
Houston Heights, 162
Houston Jones, 145
Houston Kinkaid, 145
Houston Lamar, 145, 146
Houston Lee, 147
Houston Reagan, 147, 148, 162
Houston Sam Houston, 148
Houston San Jacinto, 149
Houston St. Thomas, 149, 150
Houston Waltrip, 150, 151
Houston Wheatley, 151
Houston Worthing, 150
Houston Yates, 151, 162

I

Irving MacArthur, 75

J

Jacksonville, 98
Johnson City, 120

K

Katy, 152
Kerrville Tivy, 152
Kilgore, 98
Klein, 152

L

LaMarque, 153
Lampasas, 120
Lewisville, 75
Linden-Kildare, 99
Littlefield, 29
Longview, 99
Lubbock, 21, 22
Lubbock Monterey, 22

M

Marshall, 100, 101
Mexia, 120
Midland, 29
Midland Lee, 22
Mineola McFarland, 101
Mission, 153
Mount Vernon, 101

N

North Dallas, 61, 62
North Mesquite, 75

O

O'Donnell, 29
Odessa, 23

P

Paint Creek, 23
Pampa, 24
Paris, 102
Pearsall, 154
Perryton, 24
Pilot Point Gee, 76
Plainview, 24
Plano, 76
Port Arthur Jefferson, 154, 155
Port Isabel, 155
Post, 25

Q

Quitman, 103

R

Richardson, 76
Richardson Lake Highlands, 77
Rosenberg Lamar Consolidated, 156

S

San Angelo, 25

San Antonio Alamo Heights, 156
San Antonio Central Catholic, 157
San Antonio Cole, 157
San Antonio Houston, 157, 162
San Antonio Jefferson, 158, 159
San Antonio Southwest, 158
Santa Fe, 159
Snyder, 26
Spring Woods, 160
St. Mark's, 77, 78
Stamford, 26
Stephenville, 27
Stinnett, 27
Sugar Land, 160
Sulphur Springs, 103
Sweetwater, 27

T
Temple Dunbar, 121
Terrell, 103
Texarkana Texas, 104
Throckmorton, 28
Tyler Lee, 104
Tyler John Tyler, 105

V
Vidor, 160, 161

W
Waco, 121, 122
Weatherford, 78, 79
Wharton, 161
Wichita Falls Notre Dame, 28
Wink, 28